[redacted]

In the Absence of Bombs

Art, War, and Silence

Pascal Gielen &
Bahia Shehab (eds.)

ntennae-Arts *in* Society
liz, Amsterdam

[redacted]

the Absence of Bombs

rt, War, and Silence

scal Gielen &
hia Shehab (eds.)

[redacted]

ontributors

odul Wahhab Al-Bayati
iana Al-Halabi
uzaffar al-Nawwab
mih al-Qasim
dr Shakir al-Sayyab
mir Ashkar
mmam Azzam
n Beddegenoodts
usra Benfquih
ahmoud Darwish
lie David de Lossy
runo De Cock
lente De Keersmaeker
arlies De Munck
amiaan De Schrijver
aama Shoshana Fogiel Lewin
ra García Diaz
scal Gielen
ohamed Hijji
rwin Jans
azen Kerbaj
ra Khaldi
aha Maamoun
édecins Sans Frontières
ustafa Muftaqir
hail Salem
oschanack Shaery-Yazdi
ahia Shehab
TAN
alid Taher
na Traboulsi
mily Van Driessen
rank Vercruyssen
nnelys de Vet
aadi Youssef
amlet Zinkivskyi

[redacted]

Let Me Barbaric
Yousra Benfquih

If the native keepers of mountains, rivers, forests, and land are
    barbaric
Let me be savage

If the cradle of civilization is varnished in blood
Let me uncivil

If in the name of our Western values every ten minutes a child
Let me never be us and uncultivated

If who clings to an olive tree as if clutching their child wild
Let me be wilder

If those who with their last bread first feed the animals animal
Let me bestial

If stop apartheid and land back are too much to ask
Let me be radical

If those who resist occupation are deemed violent
Let me be militant

If media persist in a single story
Let me illiterate

If progress consists of AI-enhanced weapons of war and
    killing rates
Let me be back-to-back backwards, back to the stone ages

If those who cry over this catastrophe are called emotional
those shouting at Schuman Square or Capitol Hill hot-headed

Let me be hysterical
Let me be raging
irrational

If enlightened intellectuals speak of good versus evil,
of children of the dark and children of the light
Let me untaught, blatantly inerudite
Oh God, leave me in the dark

If in the name of the Bible the birthland of Jesus ablaze
Let me be godless, let me past all salvation

If a mass murder praised by Europe as successful
Let me be free from praise

If this is the world
Let me eternal étranger, nomad, forever not at home

If people on the run bearing white flags shot down like birds
by the sole democracy in the Middle East,
Let me be bloody undemocratic

If this is a constitutional state, the rule of law
Let me be rabble, rebellious, ungovernable

If these are your and my leaders
Yallah, let us be disobedient
untameable, undisciplined, unbridled, unruly
unyielding
unbending.

Let me barbaric

Let me unshackled beastlike beast

Let me wild through and through

Let me animal:

Let me rat,

Let me snake,

Let me ant,
those who carry up to a hundred times their weight
for the sake of the colony

Let me donkey,
heal others with my milk
still their hunger with my rump,

Let me beast
let me cloak myself in fur,
howl like a wolf.

Let me smell the way
to my beloved,
Let me inquire the way home
through the radiation of the earth,
Let me like a wild goose be
loud and long in my mourning.

Less than animal

Let me be
fungus
wiring for the whispering of trees
when fire or other dangers loom.

Let me plankton
offer you oxygen
and nourishment
for the whale whose belly no longer houses a prophet who
    will make the village see its ways
after he has been spat out on the beach
gasping for breath,
    where are the prophets
    where are the villages.

Let me be the grains of sand
beneath the saliva,

Let me be the waves
that break on the surf wildly,

Let me feral

moving to the rhythm of the moon,
being reminded of a primordial song,
an original tale,

Let me restless,

Let me wild,

Let me savage,

Let me be

barbaric.

Poet's Note

The genocide against the Palestinian people is enabled by their dehumanization—a process rooted in racism, Islamophobia, and Orientalism. Palestinian literary scholar Edward Said coined the last of these terms to describe how the West has long imagined the East as its negative mirror: while casting itself as enlightened, rational, and superior, it depicted the East as irrational, barbaric, and uncivilized, thereby legitimizing colonial conquest.

That colonial discourse persists today. The brown, Muslim—in this instance Palestinian—Other is portrayed as inherently violent or terrorist, barbaric, and savage; consequently, their systematic destruction can be rationalized in the name of 'saving Western civilization, saving the values of Western civilization', to use the words of Israeli President Herzog.

This dehumanization saturates the genocidal rhetoric of public officials who have urged that Gaza be turned into 'Auschwitz', a slaughterhouse, and who label Palestinians 'savages', 'human animals', ants, rats, snakes—even 'less than animals'.

This poem was written as a response to that wounding discourse.

—Yousra Benfquih

[redacted]

Contents

9 **Let Me Barbaric**
Yousra Benfquih

23 **Introducing Art, War, and Silence**
Bahia Shehab
Pascal Gielen

Part 1
Imagery
The Lens of Conflict

39 **Spitting Off the Edge of the World**
On the Aesthetics of Life and Death
Pascal Gielen

57 **When Art Begins to Function as a Meme, It No Longer Hurts**
Interview with Tammam Azzam
Pascal Gielen
Jan Beddegenoodts

67 **Gaza Reflections**
Mazen Kerbaj

75 **Watching War**
Marlies De Munck

93 **Bearing Witness**
The Ethics of Seeing in Humanitarian Photography
Interview with Julie David de Lossy, Bruno De Cock (Médecins Sans Frontières)
Marlies De Munck
Pascal Gielen

103 **Measures Against Violence**
Theatre in Unsettled Times
Erwin Jans

119 **Stay Upright**
An Essay and Conversation with Theatre Company STAN on European Aesthetics, Cynicism, and Morality in Times of War
Pascal Gielen

Part 2
Witnesses
Torn Between Bombs and the Absence of Bombs

133 **The Vertical Gaze**
Interview with Diana Al-Halabi
Emily Van Driessen
Jan Beddegenoodts

147 **Left Right**
Drawings and Selection of Poems
Mohamed Hijji

177 **Our Lives Have Become Lines**
Sohail Salem
Annelys de Vet

191 **And Tomorrow, We Will See Death Again**
Amir Ashkar
Jan Beddegenoodts

199 **Drawing Between the Sirens**
Making Art During Wartime, One Day at a Time
Interview with Gamlet Zinkivskyi
Jan Beddegenoodts

211 **We're Still Alive, So Remove Us from Memory**
Asynchronicity and the Museum in Resistance
Lara Khaldi

Part 3
Grief
The Art of Loss and Mourning

227 **To Break Up with I'**
Naama Shoshana Fogiel Lewin

233 **Grief and Healing amid a Genocide**
Roschanack Shaery-Yazdi

245 **When There Is No Body to Grieve For**
Lara García Diaz

261 **Black on White**
Jana Traboulsi

269 **Something Smiles Through All the Drowsiness of the World**
A Field Report
Maha Maamoun

285 **Hold on to Her**
On Grief and Ritual Justice
Pascal Gielen

292 **Drawings**
Walid Taher

295 **Contributors**

307 **Antennae-Arts *in* Society Series**

309 **Indices**

315 **Colophon**

[redacted]

Walid Taher, *You Sons of Bitches*, 2005, drawing of a working-class man screaming at the globe

ياولاد الكلب!!

Introducing Art, War, and Silence

Bahia Shehab
Pascal Gielen

Let me be
fungus
wiring for the whispering of trees
when fire or other dangers loom.

These lines, stolen from Yousra Benfquih's opening poem *Let Me Barbaric*, do not whisper, they cry. They erupt. They claw their way out of a reality too often wrapped in euphemism, too often silenced by diplomacy and the deadening language of neutrality. Benfquih's verses offer neither comfort nor resolution. They speak from and to the wound. In their invocation of wildness, animality, savagery, they reclaim what 'civilization' has tried to repress: an ethics that feels, a politics that mourns, and an aesthetics that refuses to be polite. Her poem sets the tone for this book. It kicks the door down. It is the prelude to a collective reckoning. In a time when the world seems increasingly governed by the erratic impulses of blind power—when figures like Putin, Trump, or Netanyahu turn politics into a theatre of irrational violence, when reason is hijacked by 'the crazy'—Benfquih's proposal for poetic and ethical inversion no longer feels irrational.

In the Absence of Bombs emerged from a shared disquiet. One of us returned from war-torn Ukraine with the heaviness of haunted eyes and hesitant hands; the other, from a region where art is always political, always contested, always a battleground for memory and survival. In our dialogues, we found resonance in silence—not the silence of complicity, but the silence after the blast, the silence before the scream. We found resonance in rage. And we found, across borders, bodies, and bombs, that artists persist. Even—especially—when language fails.

This book unfolds in three interwoven movements. The first, *Imagery: The Lens of Conflict*, asks how we look at war—and how artists, politicians, universities, and cultural institutions relate to it. It questions the dominant gaze and sheds light on the counter-aesthetics proposed by humanitarian workers, visual artists, theatre makers, and filmmakers. The second part, *Witnesses: Torn Between Bombs and the Absence of Bombs*, hands the word to those who live with or speak from the fissures of violence.

Artists, thinkers, and cultural workers from Lebanon, Palestine, and Ukraine—some in diaspora, others still within the war zones—bear witness not just to destruction but to the fractures of presence and absence that war inscribes in body and soul. The third and final part, *Grief: The Art of Loss and Mourning*, turns to separation and the labour of mourning. Here, scholars and artists grapple with grief—not as a private affair, but as a political and aesthetic act. Mourning becomes a method. Loss a medium.

These three parts do not speak in isolation. They reverberate—through murmur and echo, through clash and resonance. Each section offers a different angle, a different proximity to the violence that saturates our times. Together they call not only for understanding, but for an aesthetics of attention—slow and careful to dwell in the silence after the blast.

We begin with *The Lens of Conflict*. How might art see what mainstream media flattens? What visual grammars can interrupt the aesthetic of shock? We explore how painting, photography, drawing, film, and theatre become tools not just of reflection, but disruption.

While Benfquih's verses offer the emotional overture of this book, 'Spitting Off the Edge of the World' attempts to provide its conceptual scaffolding. Written in the aftermath of the full-scale invasion of Ukraine and under the shadow of Gaza, this essay investigates how the deadly logic of bureaucracy and diplomacy disarms public sensibility more effectively than war images. When images fail to move us—when repetition dulls their power—how can art still resist? The answer lies not in the egocentric gaze of the Western artist or in aestheticized neutrality, but in art that reconnects with collectivity—disoriented, embodied, affective, vulnerable. This is not an art of clear answers, but of hesitation and shared refusal. The essay proposes that resistance today demands collective rhythm and rekindled commons.

From 'Spitting Off the Edge of the World', which interrogates the aesthetics of bureaucracy and the language of control, we enter the quiet studio of Tammam Azzam, a Syrian visual artist currently based in Berlin; an artist who began as a painter but turned to digital collage when war deprived him of canvas and pigment, and later returned to painting for reasons

[redacted]

just as urgent. The digital realm allowed him to reach a global audience and express immediate anguish, but it also carried the risk of simplification and sensationalism. In our conversation, he explains that painting allows for slowness, ambiguity, and depth—qualities essential for mourning and for resisting the reduction of suffering to viral content. He resists the spectacle not through withdrawal, but by returning to a medium that requires contemplation rather than consumption. His retreat into painting after viral fame resonates with Lebanese cartoonist, trumpeter, and visual artist Mazen Kerbaj's quiet refusal in drawing. These works do not shout—they ache. They are amplified by our conversation with Julie David de Lossy and Bruno De Cock, both Belgian staff members of Médecins Sans Frontières (Doctors Without Borders), who articulate the ethical dilemmas of representing pain from within humanitarian practice. In our conversation, they reflect on the responsibility of image-makers who work in crisis zones—not only in terms of what is shown, but how, when, and for whom. They speak of the tension between visibility and dignity, the risk of retraumatizing through documentation, and the importance of consent and context. Their words resonate far beyond humanitarian work, echoing through the artistic practices collected in this book. Their critique follows after Belgian philosopher Marlies De Munck, who rewrites Sontag by insisting that images can still disturb if we dare to feel them differently. De Munck does not discard the scepticism towards media images but invites a visceral revaluation. Drawing on Judith Butler's notion of 'grievability', she suggests that even mediated images can carry affective and political power. Her essay pleads for an embodied spectatorship that remains vulnerable, that does not recoil from pain but lets it disturb the body and move it into recognition. In doing so, she returns affect to the image and insists on its capacity to rupture the anaesthesia of distance.

This act of feeling—visceral, embodied—continues with Erwin Jans, a Belgian dramaturg and theorist, in his defence of theatre as a disruptive force, where violence is not mimicked but metabolized. In 'Measures Against Violence', Jans explores how theatre, even in its apparent fragility, can resist violence by naming it, embodying it, and breaking its silence. He draws connections between political unrest and aesthetic form, questioning what theatre can do in unsettled times. Drawing on Brechtian traditions and contemporary examples of the Antwerp-based theatre Toneelhuis, he insists on theatre's ability to destabilize consensus and provoke ethical reflection. Jans reminds us that the stage, far from being a retreat, can be a front line—a space to confront, to rupture, to remember.

STAN, a Belgian theatre collective, performs resistance by staying upright in the face of collapse. In the essay and conversation 'Stay Upright', they reflect on their refusal to conform to the shock aesthetics that dominate contemporary visual and media culture. Rather than confronting violence with images of trauma or heroic declarations, they lean into fragility, irony, and ambiguity. Their stage remains bare, their gestures unheroic, their tone often laced with cynicism, even sarcasm. It raises an uncomfortable question: Is this the aesthetics we want to place in response to the violence of the world?

In the absence of bombs, do we afford ourselves the luxury of ambivalence? Is irony not a typically bourgeois mode—detached, clever, safe—built on old and new colonialism? Or could it still be a form of resistance, precisely because it holds on to nuance where the world demands sides? 'We do not take a moral high ground,' they say. 'We remain on the ground. Upright, but not elevated.' Their refusal to simplify is not indifference, but insistence: that complexity must not be surrendered, even under pressure of polarization. Their art hovers, listens, hesitates. It is, as they suggest, not a response to war, but to the ways war reshapes discourse: the flattening of language, the destruction of nuance, the replacement of complexity by slogans.

The second part, *Witnesses: Torn Between Bombs and the Absence of Bombs*, considers not only what it means to endure war, but what it means to observe it from a distance. How do artists position themselves between intimacy and estrangement, empathy, and guilt?

In her dialogue with Belgians Emily Van Driessen and Jan Beddegenoodts, Diana Al-Halabi, a Lebanese visual artist based in the Netherlands, reflects on the vertical gaze of drones

[redacted]

and surveillance. This gaze—emerging from military technology, satellites, and cameras that look down upon bodies and territories—flattens lives into targets, abstracting experience into coordinates. Al-Halabi exposes how such a gaze dehumanizes, how it erases the ground-level intimacy of lived experience and turns vision into control. Her work resists this regime of observation by reclaiming space from below, from the ground of vulnerability and resistance. In her paintings, she invites us—again and again—to look up. To turn our gaze skyward. To confront the omnipresent threat that looms above. She lets us feel, in brushstroke, what it means to live under the sky as target, as wound. In doing so, her visual language resonates with De Munck's ethical and visceral call: to not look away from the distant detonation, to allow ourselves to be disturbed by the aerial perspective of destruction. Where De Munck gives this trauma a theoretical and affective weight, Al-Halabi translates it into pigment and silence—a shared resistance to the abstraction of violence from above. This oppressive viewpoint is inverted by the poems by Mohamed Hijji, an Egyptian poet and visual artist, and Dutch designer and researcher Annelys de Vet's mappings with Sohail Salem, a Palestinian poet and educator, where horizontal lines trace displacement and care. Their collaborative cartography avoids the abstraction of geopolitical maps, instead grounding the viewer in lived experience—lines of flight become lines of intimacy, exile, and fragile connection. These drawings and poetic inscriptions record not only escape routes but also memories, gestures, and longings—rendering exile not merely as absence, but as a textured presence. Instagram fragments from Amir Ashkar, a Palestinian philosopher and writer, puncture the digital present with grief, composed in the immediacy of unfolding violence. His words, both philosophical and wounded, interrupt the scrolling eye with the unbearable weight of presence and loss. Even in their ephemerality, these posts ask us to bear witness—revealing that virtual mourning, too, leaves behind the indelible shape of a body, a name, a silence.

Gamlet Zinkivskyi, a Ukrainian street artist based in Kharkiv, known for his monochrome murals and ironic visual language, sketching in Kharkiv under bombardment, offers a fragile alternative to the heroism of resistance. His murals, often sprayed onto ruined walls in greyscale tones, reflect a melancholic humour and an irreverent tenderness that refuses to aestheticize violence. This gesture—simultaneously resilient and absurd—is itself a form of witness, one that does not scream but lingers like ash after fire. In his interview with filmmaker Jan Beddegenoodts, Gamlet speaks of art as a way to cope with the absurdity of war and the absurdity of everyday survival. Rather than grand gestures, his work captures fleeting moments—an abandoned toy, a cracked window, an overturned chair—not to monumentalize suffering, but to render it intimate, close, and painfully real. His quiet images parallel those of Kerbaj, Azzam, and Hijji—gestures not of surrender, but of staying human. Gamlet's poetic absurdism is also illustrated by a mask he commissioned from the renowned Ukrainian mask-maker Bob Basset, known for crafting striking, leather-bound masks for famous hard rock and metal bands such as Slipknot and Metallica. Basset's work bridges the line between industrial grotesque and fantastical surrealism, and his collaboration with Gamlet adds a further layer of performative contradiction to the artist's visual testimony. Gamlet wore the mask—an object as surreal as it is haunting—during his performance in Brussels. More precisely, he donned it while executing a public art commission for the European Parliament. The mask features an eerie, artificial smile: too wide, too fixed, too detached. With its grotesque grin, the mask confronted the institutional facade of neo-liberal diplomacy head-on—a theatrical response to the demand for eternal optimism that so often masks necropolitical diplomacy. The smile became a mirror: polished and grotesque. Gamlet explains that the smile is meant to express the absurd expectation of positivity in the midst of devastation—a grotesque grin forced onto a grieving face, echoing the societal pressure to carry on, to look fine, even as everything falls apart inside.

A powerful last intervention in part two comes from 'We're Still Alive, So Remove Us from Memory', a text that brings an explicitly institutional lens to the question of testimony. Lara Khaldi's contribution is the only one in this part that looks at an institution, the museum—not as neutral space for remembrance,

[redacted]

but as an active agent in forgetting, in redirecting memory, and in managing time. The Palestinian curator shows how national museums, especially in colonial and postcolonial contexts, attempt to enclose history within a fictional 'post-revolutionary' frame—while the violence of occupation or state repression remains ongoing. Her examples range from Abu Jihad's missing pistol to stories of buried treasure and secret archives, showing how material absence can become a force of narrative presence.

Against the idea of the museum as a static house of the past, she imagines the 'museum in resistance' as a generative, collective disintegration of that very logic. It is not an archive, but an act of circulation. It does not preserve, but transforms. And it resists colonial time by refusing to function as a symbol of closure. Instead, Khaldi proposes a politics of the graveyard as site of haunting, potential, and living memory. Her essay ends with a call to preserve secrets as acts of shared survival, and to imagine the commons not in a future utopia, but in the present struggle.

This reimagining of the museum as a fugitive commons—a living, encrypted network of resistance—resonates with the argument in 'Spitting Off the Edge of the World'. Both texts point to the danger of aestheticizing violence, of neutralizing pain through display, bureaucracy, or professional distance. And both return, ultimately, to the need for collective aesthesis—not spectacle, not narcissistic expression, but sensing-with-others. What is suppressed, in both cases, is the collective. What must return is the commons.

This need for commons resonates also in the final part, *Grief: The Art of Loss and Mourning*. What becomes of sorrow when its rituals are stolen? Too often, grief is psychologized, privatized, neutralized. Here, we explore how art can reclaim mourning as a collective, political, and even insurgent practice.

Naama Shoshana Fogiel Lewin, an Israeli writer and performer, writing from within the contradictions of Israeli identity, offers a searing plea to unmoor the self from the violence enacted in the name of this identity. Her contribution takes the form of a letter—one among many that have appeared as part of an ongoing performance composed of letters. This 'divorce letter' is both intimate and confrontational: a political and personal document in which she calls not only for a separation from the structures of the Israeli state, but for an internal rupture from the narratives that sustain it. Through poetic fragments and philosophical reflections, she exposes the psychological dissonance of living within an identity saturated by militarized nationalism and calls for a different form of belonging—one rooted in refusal and vulnerability.

Roschanack Shaery-Yazdi, a German Lebanese political historian, offers one of the most intimate and unsettling pieces in this book. In a deeply embodied reflection, she writes how the ongoing genocide in Gaza allowed her to finally cut the white man out of herself—the internalized figure shaped by years of working within white, Western institutions. Her essay does not merely describe mourning; it enacts it as a painful shedding of layers of complicity. Framed through a feminist lens and grounded in her own experience as a scholar and mother, she explores how grief becomes a slow, rhythmic act of endurance and resistance. She refuses to leave mourning in the private domain and instead demands its recognition as a structural, political force. In Shaery-Yazdi's hands, mourning becomes a scalpel, a soft but relentless act of undoing what whiteness has made invisible.

Lara García Diaz, a Spanish artist and cultural theorist, offers a reflection on the Spanish Civil War and her own familial legacy, revealing what happens when the state refuses to mourn its dead. Drawing on personal history—her grandfather's silence, the gaps in family memory—she examines the uneasy coexistence of forgetting and remembrance in post-Franco Spain. Her text uncovers the denial and bureaucratic erasure that surround historical violence, and asks what kinds of mourning are still possible when official narratives remain silent. It is a deeply felt meditation on grief inherited, interrupted, and reactivated across generations. Her story loops back to De Munck's gaze, to Fogiel Lewin's rupture, and to Ashkar's refusal—insisting on remembrance as rebellion. A drawing by Jana Traboulsi, a Lebanese graphic designer and illustrator, crystallizes these layers: a body, carried in silence, speaking volumes.

The final piece, 'Hold on to Her', attempts to interweave these threads. It contextualizes *hold on to her*, a film by film-

[redacted]

maker Robin Vanbesien that revisits the case of Mawda, a two-year-old Kurdish girl who was shot and killed by Belgian police during a migration control operation in 2018. The film is not built on spectacle, but on care—it offers a polyphonic, poetic investigation into the bureaucratic mechanisms surrounding Mawda's death and the muted responses of the Belgian state. The work invites viewers into the interstices of silence and responsibility, allowing voices of activists, witnesses, and mourning communities to resonate slowly and affectively. Grief, once pulled out of the isolating logic of individual psychology, can become a ritual space of collective meaning-making. It is not about closure, but about holding open what has been wounded. By treating mourning not as a private affair but as a shared practice, it's an attempt to preserve its political potency. In a time when grief is often quickly appropriated, commodified, or psychologized, *hold on to her* attempts to slow down, to listen to the dead, and to reimagine mourning as a fragile form of justice.

We offer this book as gesture. Not as answer, but as wound. And we do so with deep gratitude: to all the contributors who gave their words, images, testimonies, and time freely—with full commitment to the urgency of this project. Your generosity is etched into every page. And to our publisher, Valiz: thank you for choosing to walk this fragile, necessary path with us, for daring to make space for silences, and doubts.

It is a book that whispers. That rages. That remembers. And that desperately tries to understand what is going on. Neither in theory, nor in the empirical, but through aesthesis: through all our senses and affects.

Let us be unruly
Let us be barbaric
Perhaps a way to stay upright

—Bahia Shehab & Pascal Gielen,
June 2025, Cairo & Antwerp

[redacted]

Walid Taher, *Flammable Material*, 2011, drawing of the working class walking with their heads down

مواد مشتعلة

Part 1
Imagery

The Lens of Conflict

[redacted]

Spitting Off the Edge of the World

On the Aesthetics of Life and Death

Pascal Gielen

Cowards, here's the sun
So bow your heads
In the absence of bombs
Draw your breath
Dark, dark places shall be none
She's melting houses of gold
We're spitting off the edge of the world
—Yeah Yeah Yeahs & Perfume Genius

Haunted Eyes

'Spitting Off the Edge of the World'—a rather pathetic pop song, its lyrics quite sentimental, and yet... it echoes persistently in my mind. Perhaps I've become too affected after my journey through full-scale war in Ukraine. It wasn't the bombed-out houses or the mutilated bodies that etched into me. It was something far more elusive. A visceral expression, unspoken, etched into the faces of soldiers, artists, journalists, children—ordinary people like you and me. Eyes darkened by fear, trauma, anger, frustration, helplessness. A gaze that seemed to carry an unbearable weight of liminality.

Spitting—a defiant, desperate gesture. An act that embodies both rejection and assertion, primal in its simplicity. At the edge of the world, where there is no solid ground to cling to, only the abyss. Hells on earth. Gaza, torn apart between Israel and the United States. Ukraine, crushed between Russia and Europe—or better, between Russia and the US again. Like so many liminal spaces around the globe, trapped between forces far greater than themselves, offering no certainties, no guarantees. Spitting becomes an existential act: a declaration of dignity in the face of obliteration. Perhaps it is not merely defiance, but an assertion of humanity in a world that seeks to strip it away. Even when the ground beneath you crumbles, spitting declares: 'I am here. I refuse to disappear'. It is a small rebellion, one that may dissolve into the void, but nonetheless affirms the stubborn persistence of being human. The creeping awareness of powerlessness. The haunting suspicion that none of it will matter.

Resistance is essential, yet inaction feels like complicity. And still, you cannot shake the thought: Does it make any difference at all? In the strained faces I recognized this tension—an unbearable in-betweenness. In the trembling hands, the restless movements, the haunted eyes. Bodies not physically broken, but mentally cursed. These were not defeated bodies, yet neither were they triumphant. They hovered in a space between action and despair, between survival and surrender.

This sensory experience crawled under my skin. I cannot shake it. Perhaps it's the result of what could be called an 'aesthetic experience of war'. A confrontation where all the senses collide and distort, mingling with one's affective system. Safe at home, no media image can replicate this. The stark numbers of casualties and the calculated analyses of geopolitical strategies fail even more to touch me. These abstractions lack the visceral impact, the unbearable immediacy of the pain of others.

As Susan Sontag writes in *Regarding the Pain of Others*, images are handicapped in their ability to convey the essence of war. A photograph of destruction may shock, but prolonged exposure often leads to numbness. Such images rarely incite political action or lasting engagement, particularly in places where the bombs are absent. Repeated exposure to suffering can paradoxically desensitize us, replacing urgency with apathy. This is because images are merely fragments of reality—snapshots stripped of their context and nuance.

For Sontag, pictures can haunt us, but the moral impact of war photography depends on the narratives that accompany it. Without these narratives, images remain superficial provocations, momentary disruptions that quickly fade. Compassion is fleeting. It must translate into action, or it withers, leaving only indifference in its wake. In a world oversaturated with visuals, this paradox renders images impotent. They fail to pierce the comfortable detachment of those untouched by conflict.

So, if neither rational arguments nor emotive images can stir us, what can? What aesthetics remain that might truly shake us out of our indifference? What kind of art, what kind of words, sounds, or gestures, can breach the cold armour of diplomacy we can hear in recent years at our universities, cultural organizations, and public institutions?

These questions linger, pressing and unresolved. But to answer them, we must first grasp the very thing we seek to confront: the logic of today's bureaucratic reason, that inhuman machinery of calculation and efficient diplomacy.

The Beauty of Neutrality

After my experiences in a war zone, the endless scheming, equivocation, and double-speak became increasingly jarring to my ears. The perpetual blowing of hot and cold. Following Hamas' attack on 7 October 2023, this ambivalence crystallized into a diplomatic mantra, a bureaucratic rationale wherein the word 'neutrality' was invoked as if it could exorcise all evils.

After the renewed escalation of the Israeli-Palestinian conflict, the University of Antwerp, with which I am affiliated, suddenly began to second-guess its earlier, resolute support for Ukraine. According to its mission statement, the university must distinguish itself from activist groups by 'cherishing the plurality of perspectives inherent to scientific methods'. My rector at the time used this same mission to justify his refusal to take an official stance on Gaza. The policy swiftly translated into action when several students were reprimanded for organizing a demonstration for Palestine on campus. University regulations, it seems, forbid the use of campus spaces for 'activities of a purely party-political nature or one-sided political propaganda'.

In an email to staff, the rector stated that the university strives to be a 'politically neutral and safe space for dialogue and debate'. According to him, students and staff feel unsafe when a university 'takes a side'. Neutrality, then, was framed as a guarantor of safety.

And yet, only a few months earlier, far-right Flemish politician Filip Dewinter had been granted permission to present his book *Omvolking* (population replacement) in that very same building. Apparently, he had complied with the formal procedures for reserving a venue. A case, perhaps, of the letter of the law prevailing over its spirit?

The rector defended this act of hospitality with a familiar refrain: 'Freedom of speech is the cornerstone of democracy'. Notably, there was no mention of safety at the time. One can't help but ask: Who, precisely, is afforded the right to feel safe within the university's walls? Even setting that aside, can neutrality ever truly safeguard us? When all voices are silenced in the name of balance, do the ghosts not haunt us all the more? Especially when Sontag's media images continue to haunt us beyond the university's walls.

What surprised me most, however, was that this rhetoric of safety and neutrality came from a pacifist, a quite progressive rector—a historian who had conducted research on the Holocaust and Jewish persecution. How could such a morally engaged intellectual find himself ensnared in the cold calculus of this bureaucratic rationale?

There is, of course, a very good reason why a rector would resort to this raison. Bureaucracy has a very special quality. In its ideal form, it is one of modernity's greatest gifts. Within a democracy, it ensures that all are treated equitably and that everyone stands equal before the law. Positions are awarded based on merit, not lineage; rules and qualifications, not bloodlines, determine leadership. In this ideal world, bureaucracy embodies the beauty of neutrality.

Sociologist Max Weber recognized the duality as early as the twentieth century. Bureaucracy brings order and rationality to the murky waters of power and ambition. It replaces whims with rules, chaos with clarity. But Weber also noted that bureaucracy has its roots in the military. Violence, then, is written into its very DNA. Its efficiency, precision, and hierarchies mirror those of the barracks. Orders flow downward, unquestioned, while accountability is diffused across countless layers.

Weber's famous 'iron cage'—paperwork as violence. Not overt or physical violence, but something more insidious and soul-crushing: a violence against purpose, against creativity. Bureaucracy compels; it does not negotiate. Its commands, unrelenting and blind, resonate with the authoritarian orders of a battlefield. Farmers, teachers, healthcare workers—all find themselves today conscripted into this labyrinthine system.

Bureaucracy does not ask; it demands. Herein lies its betrayal of humanity: in its relentless pursuit of efficiency, it objectifies individuals, reducing them to mere data points. To objectify is, in a sense, to kill subjectivity—to suppress the unique, the exceptional, the irreplaceable, and the creative spark of life in every person. Bureaucracy exhales an aesthetics of death.

The Banality of Killing

Hannah Arendt draws another connection between bureaucracy and death. In her book *Eichmann in Jerusalem*, she introduced the controversial concept of the 'banality of evil'. Adolf Eichmann, the Nazi bureaucrat responsible for emigration and deportation, was not a bloodthirsty fanatic. He was a figure of dreary mediocrity: dutiful, thoughtlessly zealous, and committed not to ideology but to the art of efficient task execution. Evil, Arendt argued, does not need monstrous intent. It flourishes in the cold abstraction of bureaucracy, where human suffering is reduced to mere lines in a ledger.

Bureaucracy, then, becomes the perfect accomplice to oppressive regimes. It cloaks violence in the guise of neutrality, executing necro-diplomacy through measured calculations. Institutional professionals, loyal not to people but to systems, embody this chilling indifference. Consider, for instance, my university rector's response to a petition signed by 7,000 Belgian academics calling for a boycott of Israeli universities: 'Ceasing Horizon research projects with Israeli institutions would cost the University of Antwerp 2.1 million euros. And we don't have that money.'

The tone was calm and pragmatic. And there lies the violence. How many deaths in Palestine must we tally before we dare call it genocide? For the bureaucratic mind, mass murder is merely semantics—a product of precise definitional arithmetic.

Arendt's analysis of Eichmann warns us that this logic is no relic. It festers in every institution where efficiency serves as a shield for complicity. Bureaucratic reasoning even ensnared Jewish councils (*Judenräte*) during the Holocaust. The Nazis coerced these councils into compiling deportation lists, confiscating property, and maintaining order, offering them an illusion of control. Many Jewish leaders justified their co-operation with this dark practice of *Auskämmen* (combing out) with the chilling logic: sacrificing thousands to save hundreds. But collaboration only smoothed the machinery of genocide. Had the Jewish councils resisted, even imperfectly, the Nazi machine might have stumbled. Resistance, however flawed, could have saved half of the six million Jewish lives, Arendt claimed.

This analysis cost Arendt dearly; she lost many friends and allies. Yet her warning remains brutally clear: bureaucracy—indifferent, efficient, and amoral—is the staunchest ally of inhuman regimes. Its cold logic seeps into those who dwell too long in its corridors, whether they are Nazi officers, university rectors, or directors of cultural and public institutions who prioritize their organizations and their own positions over humanity.

Creative Industries of War

Leading polyvocal institutions is, of course, no easy task. It requires diplomacy, constant manoeuvring, and a talent for juggling. One might even feel a certain sympathy for such balancing acts. Rectors or directors of public institutions, after all, occupy positions of authority. What is striking, however, is that not only these officials but also independent writers, filmmakers, and academics—often of a more progressive persuasion, sometimes self-declared pacifists or activists—suddenly fall silent, particularly when it comes to Palestine. At other times, their radical activism dissolves into vague talk of 'neutrality' once again. When even creative, free-thinking minds are affected by this bureaucratic rationale, there must be more compelling reasons. Why this wavering?

Guilt, perhaps? In Germany, for instance, any critique of Israel is swiftly branded as anti-Semitic. This bad conscience runs deep, likely across much of Europe. Among the progressive descendants of former collaborators, in particular, the spectre of the Final Solution continues to haunt. But could this truly explain their averted gaze from Netanyahu's mass lynchings? For artists and intellectuals, such an irrational act of 'atonement' seems uncharacteristic. Perhaps this incantation of neutrality by the

[redacted]

progressive camp is instead directed at different spectres.

Another oft-invoked justification is economic in nature. Companies, universities, and cultural institutions are reluctant to endanger their ties with Israeli partners, and therefore cling to what is conveniently termed a 'neutral' stance. Borrowing from Nancy Fraser, this semblance of neutrality might more accurately be described as progressive neo-liberalism—an ideology that fuses the rhetoric of progressive social movements, such as feminism, multiculturalism, or environmentalism, with the imperatives of neo-liberal market logic. It enables individuals, institutions, and corporations to perform social awareness while firmly securing their allegiance to capital and competition. One might just as well think of that regiment of Magnum photographers, dispatching shocking images across the globe. Are they moved by commitment—or by commission? Do they act in the name of humanity, or for the benefit of their own portfolios? In that light, even the rector's diplomatically phrased sum of 2.1 million euros fits rather snugly within this lucrative logic. A price tag, perhaps, for principle.

Progressive neo-liberalism thrives by co-opting the language of activism and justice, transforming it into a tool for economic gain. Feminism is embraced, but only insofar as it supports 'lean-in' corporate success stories. Cultural diversity is celebrated, but only when it bolsters a company's brand or profitability. Even activism is commodified, marketed as a lifestyle choice rather than a call for systemic change. As Fraser argues, this alignment of progressive values with neo-liberal priorities creates a system that appears inclusive and ethical on the surface, while perpetuating the very structural inequalities it claims to oppose.

In today's cultural sphere and the art world, activism is decidedly 'in'—at least in its discursive form. Supporting progressive causes has become a profitable enterprise, a means of accruing cultural and economic capital. Consider, for instance, the creative industries built around the Second World War. This memory industry has been operating at full tilt for decades, churning out novels, films, and exhibitions that transform historical trauma into consumable narratives. These cultural products are often marketed as moral imperatives, necessary acts of remembrance, while simultaneously generating substantial profits.

Take, for example, *Wil* by Belgian writer Jeroen Olyslaegers or *War and Turpentine* by Stefan Hertmans. Through the lens of morally ambiguous protagonists, these novels explore complicity, guilt, and resistance during the German occupation of Belgium. While they offer nuanced meditations on wartime ethics, they also capitalize on the enduring fascination with this historical period, drawing readers to the gravity of their subject matter. Likewise, Hollywood has long mastered the art of transforming the atrocities of the Second World War into box-office hits. Films such as *Schindler's List*, *The Pianist*, and *Jojo Rabbit* blend historical gravitas with compelling storytelling, rendering a horrifying past both palatable and profitable.

These works are not inherently problematic; indeed, they often serve as vital vehicles for education and reflection. Yet their success underscores the dual nature of cultural production within a neo-liberal framework: the capacity to generate both moral authority and economic profit. By contrast, taking a stand on the Palestinian issue risks alienating audiences or offending financial stakeholders, thereby diminishing income. Activism's stakes thus become calculable, not in terms of justice but in terms of profit and loss. Consequently, many so-called engaged authors, artists, and filmmakers suddenly find themselves silent when it comes to Palestine.

And herein lies the paradox of progressive neo-liberalism: it allows artists, war photographers, and institutions to espouse progressive values when it is convenient—or profitable to do so—while avoiding any gesture that might truly unsettle the economic status quo. In this way, activism itself is commodified, its radical edge dulled, repackaged, and made palatable for consumption.

War Lab

But as any war zone, 'Lab Palestine' is also a goldmine for another reason: its profitable ventures in war and surveillance technologies, including the burgeoning AI industry. Here, real people once again serve as test subjects. War, as ever, drives innovation,

[redacted]

and for over seventy years, the Palestinian territories have been a proving ground for new technologies—whether for military purposes or later for creative industries. Many academics, entrepreneurs, and creative professionals willingly wrap themselves in a veil of ignorance, soothing their guilty consciences with chants of neutrality. Call it 'opportunistic Zen Buddhism'—a convenient detachment masking deeper complicities.

Economic entanglement sheds light on why companies, educational institutions, cultural organizations, and individual artists refrain from taking a stance. Relationships with countries in states of war are often lucrative, and neutrality offers a way to avoid disruption. Progressive neo-liberalism aptly captures this facade: an ideology that enthusiastically embraces social engagement, so long as it aligns with economic interests and safeguards careers.

Thus, liminal war zones at the edges of the world remain testing grounds not only for technology and creativity but also for the moral elasticity of institutions and individuals, including artists, war journalists, and intellectuals. The ultimate spectre of capitalism ensures that even the most progressive activism is commodified and stripped of its transformative potential. It becomes yet another product in a marketplace that thrives on exploitation, all the while cloaking itself in the language of ethics and innovation. But is it then, once again, all the fault of the ever-returning ghost, the spirit of capitalism?

Herd Individualism

Beneath Fraser's concept of 'progressive neo-liberalism' lurks yet another spectre. Beyond questions of conscience and economic incentives, cultural motives may also play a role—taboos that continue to obstruct us while they are still allowed to persist in places like Palestine and Ukraine. Neo-liberalism, after all, thrives on a cunning redefinition of freedom. More than traditional liberalism, this 'new freedom' is framed in competitive and individualistic terms. 'Being yourself' has become almost a moral imperative, especially for Western artists who remain steeped in the romanticism of the bourgeois genius. Freedom must be earned, and above all, you must fight for your own freedom, and you need to suffer for it.

This brings us to one of neo-liberalism's most insidious paradoxes: individualism, particularly its expressive variant, is no longer a personal choice but a collectively imposed obligation. You must be creative. You must be authentic. This mandate weighs heavily on artists, but also on war reporters: they are expected not only to bear witness to breaking news, but to do so with an image marked by personal flair—original, striking, unmistakably theirs.

Yet this imperative of self-expression is confined within a competitive straitjacket. Excellence is flattened, evaluated by standards dictated by the market and the media circus. Neo-liberalism pushes us towards a schizophrenic condition: you must forge your own personality—but all at once. Everyone for themselves, yet all moving in the same direction. Cultivate your authentic self—just make sure you do it in the same rhythm of the algorithm.

In the end, this highly prized individualism turns out to be nothing more than advanced collectivism. It's like the emperor's new clothes: beneath the most 'authentic' outfit hides a naked body adorned with collectively valued brands. In short, individualism becomes herd mentality, but one that must suppress its dependence on the herd. The competitive individualist is continually forced to drive their social being out of their own body. Just as the 'genius artist' or today's creative entrepreneur must constantly deny that much of their creativity is drawn from others.

This kind of exorcism ultimately leads to loneliness and mental illness. It is no surprise that Western societies rely on an army of psychiatrists and therapists. The Self Society is, after all, a hysterical society. Hysteria arises, for example, when you feel replaceable and discover that you may not be as authentic as you thought. To be unique is hell in a hypercompetitive society where there is always someone ready to knock your unique self from its pedestal. It leads to fear, distrust, and xenophobia. In the frenzy of the hysterical rat race, social Darwinism and theories of competitive genes easily merge with near-eugenic notions of white supremacy. This likely also explains the difference in Western attitudes towards Ukraine and Palestine.

What happens when members of a tormented, hyper-individualized society are confronted with people who still possess what they themselves have lost? How bitter must it feel to witness a sense of community in others—in religions, in traditions, in societies where collectivity is still allowed to matter? Has our fear of losing individuality mutated into a phobia of anything that carries the scent of collectivism? The same fear that once sparked witch hunts against communists in the so-called 'free' West may now fuel the fire of Islamophobia.

Even when we seek to evoke empathy for victims, war photographers and film-makers most often turn to the individual portrait, the personal testimony. Collective suffering rarely makes it into the frame—we no longer know how to represent it. And when the collective does appear, it is shattered, lifeless, already extinguished: the mass grave.

Could this failure to depict the collective be a symptom of our own uncertainty? A reflection of our unease, even our resentment, towards those who are still permitted to inhabit a communal spirit? Admittedly, I am speculating here, wandering into the deeper folds of our shared social unconscious. But hasn't collectivism, in our I-centred society, become something abject—something repellent, feared, cast out? A spectral presence that must be amputated again and again, lest it disrupt the neo-liberal order we are made to embody? And yet, in Palestine—and yes, also in Ukraine, suspended as it is between the legacy of communism and the lure of egocentric capitalism—a resilient collective spirit endures.

The more we bomb, colonize, terrorize, and individualize—and the louder the mantras of neutrality and bureaucratic logic resound—the more our frustration deepens. And the more relentlessly that communal force rises, confronting our individualistic psychosis—not only from beyond our borders, but from deep within our cultures and bodies. Solidary yet furious, tender yet unrelenting, like a monster we ourselves have birthed, it exposes the very root of our condition: we are, despite everything, fundamentally interdependent beings. And so, the question arises: Can image-makers also develop strategies and aesthetics to escape this condition?

Keep on Spitting

What kind of aesthetics, image, sound, or word can still move us? In a world where bureaucratic reasoning tightens its grip with insidious persistence, how do we pierce its cold, calculated logic? Are there forms of representation potent enough to resist the anesthetizing spectacle of war, the cynical choreography of neutrality, and the psychologization of collective trauma? Can artistic tools still unsettle the numbness of our psychotic individualism—this hollowed-out sense of self that neo-liberalism so carefully crafts? Or are we placing an impossible burden on the shoulders of artists, asking them to redeem what society itself no longer dares to confront?

And yet, they try. Artists keep spitting—not in rage, but in resilience. Their gestures are often small, fragile, trembling at the edge of meaning. But they resist nonetheless. Take, for instance, Johan Grimonprez' *Shadow World*. It does not seduce with spectacle. Instead, it dissects. No montage of bombed landscapes or crying children, but a slow, forensic peeling back of layers. The film reveals how corruption is not a byproduct of the global arms trade—it is its very engine. Politicians, rather than representing our hopes, become sales agents of fear. War is not a tragic failure of diplomacy, but its ultimate success under capitalism. *Shadow World* names this monstrous logic and dares to visualize the bureaucrats and lobbyists who lubricate it. It offers no catharsis, no heroes—only the dead weight of a system working exactly as intended.

But is unmasking enough? Once, perhaps, it was. Enlightenment strategies of truth-telling aimed to spark resistance by exposing hidden violence. Today, however, the violence is no longer hidden. It is broadcast live, monetized, memed. We know exactly what is happening. We see the numbers, the faces, the rubble. And we keep scrolling. Truth no longer ignites revolt—it generates content. Even horror has been formatted to fit our feeds. Neo-liberalism has not only corrupted our systems, but hollowed out our affective lives. It has normalized the unimaginable and turned complicity into the ambient noise of our daily routines.

[redacted]

So, we turn to images, again—desperate for something that might still sting. But most fail to breach the polished armour of our disbelief. They arrive pre-digested, accompanied by hashtags and streaming links, designed to shock just enough but never too much. The aesthetic of suffering has been flattened, monetized, turned into clickbait. We do not look away because it is too painful. We look away because it no longer surprises us. The personalized account, the tearful testimony, the lone survivor—all moving, all important, but so often severed from their collective and systemic frame. The war becomes an anecdote. Genocide becomes a glitch in the algorithm. Just as Sontag feared, we feel too little, too briefly—and then we feel nothing at all.

And yet, there are exceptions. In *Looking for Empathy*, Jan Beddegenoodts and Chokri Ben Chikha search for something beyond the spectacle—something less showy and more uncertain. The film follows Ben Chikha as he wanders through Israel and the occupied Palestinian territories in preparation for his theatre piece *Persians: Triumph of Empathy*. What begins as a politically engaged performance project becomes an uncomfortable reflection on the limits of empathy itself. Is it even possible to empathize with the adversary, with the occupier? And what happens when the artist becomes implicated—when the ethical line between witness and profiteer begins to blur?

By the end, Ben Chikha stands alone. The film leaves him—and us—without resolution. Not because it fails to take a position, but because it refuses to offer the comfort of clarity. It critiques not only the geopolitical machinery but also the artist's own gaze, his place in the chain of representation and commodification. It dares to ask: Is this art, or another way to polish the ego? Another project to fill the portfolio? Sontag's warning lingers here too: What if the artist, in the act of showing suffering, unwittingly neutralizes it?

This is precisely what makes Beddegenoodts' documentaries so unsettling. He does not play the neutral observer. He immerses, implicates, oscillates. Between front lines and dance floors, checkpoints and concerts. His films are not objects of knowledge but spaces of confusion—where love and hate, justice and guilt, life and death intermingle in unpredictable ways. It is an aesthetic of disorientation, where no position is safe, and no narrative is stable. This refusal of certainty is its own form of protest. Against the spreadsheet logic of diplomacy. Against the metrics of engagement. Against the sanitized image. And crucially, against the emotional dullness Sontag feared—a numbness born of endless repetition without consequence.

Heddy Honigmann's *Crazy* achieves something similar—but with silence, with stillness. Through intimate interviews with Dutch soldiers haunted by their experiences in Srebrenica, she forgoes all spectacle. No battlefield shots, no dramatic reenactments. Only talking heads—and even those seem too heavy for their own necks. The trauma is not narrated; it trembles just beneath the voice. The eyes flicker. The jaw clenches. A finger twitches. This is the language of bodies, not scripts. The war has moved in. It lives in their flesh.

Crazy creates a space where vulnerability is not exploited, but shared. Where grief is not turned into narrative but held in suspension. It does not ask us to understand war, but to feel its residue. It is, in its own quiet way, a devastating indictment of the bureaucratic chain of command—the orders that were followed, the ethics that were swallowed. This is what Arendt meant by the banality of evil: the violence of the checkbox, the daily report, the airstrike request form, the neutrality directive, the duty roster, the evacuation log. Not the bullet, but the protocol; not hatred, but the chain of command. *Crazy* makes us sit with its aftershocks. Not through horror, but through intimacy. And unlike the images Sontag distrusted—those that shock but do not move—it holds our gaze, gently but insistently, until something breaks through.

And perhaps, in that combination, we can find a way out of the aesthetic deadlock. A triangulation of strategies: a poetics of exposure (*Shadow World*), a politics of disorientation (*Looking for Empathy*), and an aesthetics of embodied trauma (*Crazy*). None of these works offers a final answer. But together, they form a constellation of refusal. A refusal to be neutral. A refusal to simplify. A refusal to numb. Grimonprez names the monster, Beddegenoodts dances with it, Honigmann listens to its breath.

And perhaps it is Beddegenoodts, most of all, who

[redacted]

points towards something new: in his montage, rhythm becomes a form of mobilization. His VJ-like editing doesn't just show the world—it pushes the viewer through it. Not towards resolution, but towards movement. And that rhythm no longer addresses or represents the isolated individual, as so often happens in neo-liberal image culture. The beat is no longer yours—it is ours. It calls the collective into motion. Not the solitary subject, but the shared pulse. Not a selfie, but a selfless sync. His films do not end in mourning; they end in momentum. Knowledge turns into energy. Grief into action. A beat. A rave. A raid. A step into the street. This is not the pessimism of mourning, but the joy of defiance. A vitalistic aesthetics, animated by a will to live that refuses to be proceduralized, neutralized, bureaucratized. An aesthetics that keeps on spitting—even when the world goes numb.

References

- Arendt, Hannah. *Eichmann in Jerusalem: A Report on the Banality of Evil.* New York: Viking Press, 1963.
- Beddegenoodts, Jan, and Chokri Ben Chikha. *Looking for Empathy.* Film. Hakuna Productions, 2024.
- Fraser, Nancy. *The Old is Dying and the New Cannot Be Born: From Progressive Neoliberalism to Trump and Beyond.* New York: Verso, 2017.
- Gielen, Pascal. *Trust: Building on the Cultural Commons.* Amsterdam: Valiz, 2023.
- Grimonprez, Johan. *Shadow World.* Film. Louverture Films, 2016.
- Hertmans, Stefan. *War and Turpentine.* Trans. David McKay. New York: Pantheon Books, 2016. Originally published in 2013.
- Honigmann, Heddy. *Crazy.* Film. VPRO Television, 1999.
- Kafka, Franz. *The Trial.* Trans. Edwin Muir and Willa Muir. Berlin: Schocken Books, 1925.
- Olyslaegers, Jeroen. *Wil.* Amsterdam: De Bezige Bij, 2016.
- Sontag, Susan. *Regarding the Pain of Others.* New York: Farrar, Straus and Giroux, 2003.
- Weber, Max. *Economy and Society: An Outline of Interpretive Sociology.* Eds. Guenther Roth and Claus Wittich. Berkeley: University of California Press, 1922.

[redacted]

When Art Begins to Function as a Meme, It No Longer Hurts

Interview with Tammam Azzam

Pascal Gielen
Jan Beddegenoodts

Tammam Azzam, from the *Storeys* series, 2015, acrylic on canvas, 170 x 190 cm

In late March 2025, we met Syrian artist Tammam Azzam at his studio in Berlin. Known for his powerful visual language that fuses memory, destruction, and resistance, Azzam's work has captured global attention since the start of the Syrian revolution in 2011.

After graduating from the Faculty of Fine Arts in Damascus in 2001, he spent a decade building an artistic practice rooted in the local context—until war and repression forced him into exile.

Over the years, Azzam's work evolved from fragile watercolours and collage-based installations to bold digital compositions that gained international acclaim, particularly his Syrian Museum series, in which iconic Western artworks are layered over photographs of bombed-out Syrian cities. In this act, Azzam staged a confrontation not only between histories of violence, but between aesthetic perception and political neglect.

In February 2025, just weeks before our conversation, Azzam returned to Syria for the first time in many years—shortly after the long-standing regime of President Assad had collapsed. The emotional charge of this return was still palpable during our exchange.

We found Tammam to be an exceptionally kind and generous host, offering us tea and time, but also something more precious: an openness to speak warmly and reflectively about his work, his memories, and the ethical tensions he continues to navigate as a Syrian artist working in the Western art world.

As we settled into his quiet, light-filled studio, surrounded by fragments of new works and remnants of past ones, we began with a question that touches the very core of his practice: What does it mean to create art as someone who carries the experience of war?

Your work often evokes a sense of stillness and fragility. What does it mean to create art as someone who carries the experience of war? Is it a form of resistance, remembrance, or refuge?

Tammam Azzam • To create art after war is to work from a silence that never leaves you. And I don't mean silence as peace, but the silence that arrives after the blast. That strange emptiness when you no longer hear the world, but you still feel its shock. That's the moment I try to capture in my work—not the explosion, not the act of violence itself, but the seconds just after. The void. The stillness. The fragility of everything that once was.
For me, that's not just aesthetic—it's personal. When I left Syria in 2011, after ten years of working in Damascus, I arrived in Dubai without a proper studio, without materials, and with a mind full of grief and confusion. All I had was my laptop. So I began working digitally—not because I had a vision, but because I had no other tools. That limitation turned into a language.
People often ask whether my work is resistance. Sometimes it is. But I don't think of resistance in slogans or messages. I think of it as a refusal. A refusal to forget. A refusal to stay silent. And also a refuge. A place where I can explore what cannot be said, where I can remain honest without having to be clear.

Let's talk about the Syrian Museum *series. You layered famous Western masterpieces over images of Syrian destruction. Why that visual strategy?*

TA • It began with Goya. I was looking at *The third of May* and thought: this could be Aleppo. The uniforms may have changed, but the scene hasn't. The story of violence against unarmed people—it repeats endlessly. That's what struck me. Not just the horror of the past, but its persistence. So I started inserting these canonical works—paintings that represent European suffering—into the ruins of Syria.

[redacted]

At first, I didn't do this as a critique of the West. It was more about creating continuity. These are global images of pain. But, of course, the reception turned political. The works began to travel. And people began to project onto them. When *The Kiss*—a digital collage of Klimt's iconic image layered on a ruined facade—went viral, it disturbed me. Not because it became known, but because people started to see only the aesthetic, the romance. They didn't see the destruction underneath.

That's when I realized: when art begins to function as a meme, it no longer hurts. It loses its ethical edge. It no longer makes you pause. And that's when I stopped the series.

What can painting do that media images can't?

TA • A media image is fast. It's consumed in seconds. You scroll, you react, you move on. But a painting insists. It stays in front of you. It demands time and attention. And it carries presence. It's not just about seeing. It's about standing still in front of a moment that refuses to fade.

When I started translating journalistic images into acrylic paintings, I was trying to reclaim time. To slow everything down. I needed to process what I was seeing in a tactile way. With brushes. With colour. With breath. Painting lets me transform the quick pain of a photograph into a durable, physical object. Something you can return to. Something that keeps asking you to remember.

I think that's what media images often fail to do. They inform, yes. But they don't ask you to live with the pain. Painting does.

Much of your work deals not with what is seen, but with what is missing: displaced bodies, silenced voices, collapsed architecture. Why this focus on absence?

TA • Absence is what stays. It lingers after everything else has fallen. I've always been drawn to ruined places—land-

scapes where human life is no longer visible, but where its trace remains. In the broken buildings, in the scattered objects, in the colours of a vanished sky.
Including human figures in my work often feels too direct. Too heavy. It's not that I don't want to show people—I do. But representing a figure, especially a victim, is incredibly difficult. It risks turning a person into a symbol. And I don't want to objectify pain.
So instead, I create the atmosphere of what's left behind. The empty streets. The debris. The colour of a place remembered. That's where the story lives for me—in what's no longer there.

How do you position yourself between silence and statement, especially in European institutional contexts that often demand one or the other?

TA • This is something I think about constantly. In some settings, people want clarity. They want to know: Is this work political or not? Does it support a position? And in other places, there's pressure to remain neutral. To aestheticize pain, but not to name it.

Do you ever worry that the beauty of your work might soften the horror behind it?

TA • Beauty can be deceptive. It can turn suffering into something palatable. But it can also hold pain in ways that make it visible again. I work with fragile materials—paper, thread, dust—because that's how I feel. That's how exile feels. And I try not to make beauty for its own sake, but as a form of honesty.
There's a quietness in ruins. A dignity even. I want to honour that. Not by reproducing horror, but by creating a space where it can be remembered.

How do you reflect on your role as a Syrian artist working in the European art world? Do you feel seen? Or instrumentalized?

TA • This is the most difficult part. I know that I am often seen as a 'Syrian artist'. That label travels with me. It opens doors, but it also fixes me in a certain frame. When people come to my exhibitions, they often want the war. They want the narrative of suffering. And that's painful. Because I'm not just that.

I want to be an artist—someone who speaks about destruction, yes, but also about light. About memory. About life. The art world has embraced my work, but sometimes I wonder: Are they embracing the pain or the person?

Looking ahead, what role can art play in post-war societies?

TA • Art can't rebuild buildings. But it can rebuild memory. It can hold grief. It can offer a space for mourning that isn't political, but personal. And sometimes, that's what people need most—not explanations, not programmes, but a place to sit with their loss.

I don't know what the future of Syria looks like. But I know that if it is to have a future, it must begin with remembering. And maybe, in some quiet way, art can help us do that.

In some of your works, the road appears as a central visual element, stretching out towards a distant horizon that often ends in a wall. What does this recurring motif of the road mean to you, particularly in works like The Road *(2015)?*

TA • *The Road,* for me, is about possibility—but also about betrayal. It's about the dream of movement, of freedom, of going somewhere, only to find that it leads to a dead end. In *The Road*, I created this long narrow path that seems to vanish into the horizon, but instead crashes into a wall. There's no exit. No continuation. Just a stop. A brutal one.

That image came from the reality of exile—of being constantly in transit, but never truly arriving. For many Syrians, and for many others around the world, the road is not a metaphor. It's lived. It's the desert road to Jordan. The sea crossing to Europe. The corridor between camps. And very often, it ends not in safety, but in more borders, more walls.

I keep returning to the road because I'm still on it. Not geographically, maybe—but emotionally. The blocked horizon is the world I come from. And still, I paint it. Still, I walk it. Because even when there's no way forward, the road reminds me: we tried.

And trying, in itself, matters.

[redacted]

Gaza Reflections

Mazen Kerbaj

[redacted]

This collection of illustrations by Lebanese cartoonist, trumpeter and visual artist Mazen Kerbaj captures the raw emotions felt after we started seeing footage come out of Gaza. It reflects the early sentiments of many people who realized that the Israeli invasion of Gaza was a genocide, from as early as October 2023.

Mazen Kerbaj, *Gaza 17 October 2023*, 2023, ink on paper

Mazen Kerbaj, *When I Was a Kid*, 2023, ink on paper

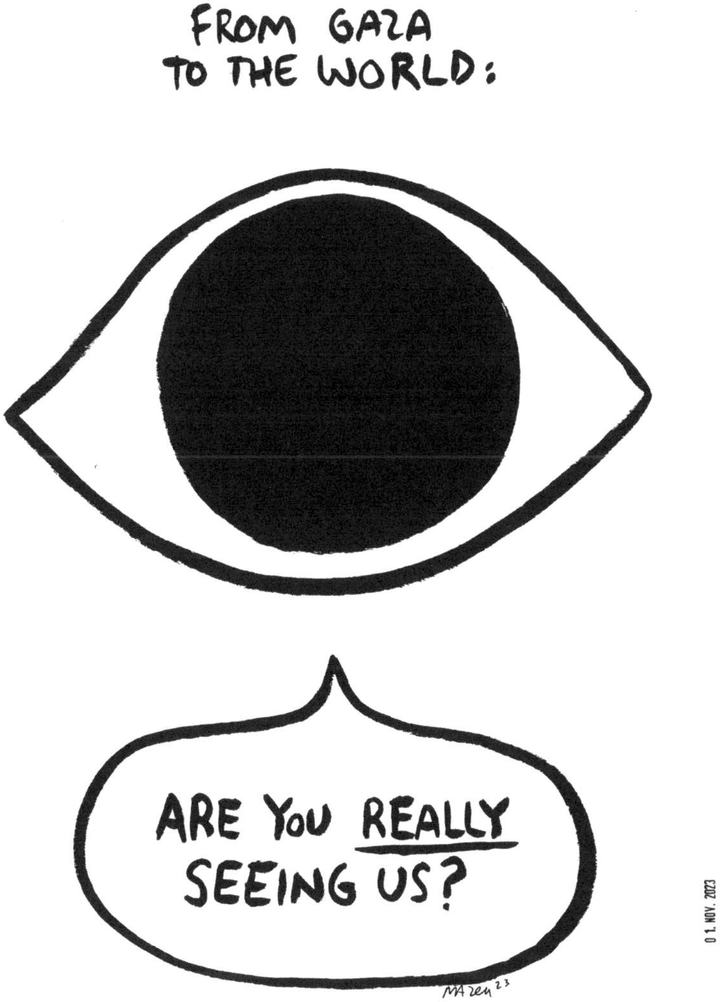

Mazen Kerbaj, *From Gaza to the World*, 2023, ink on paper

Mazen Kerbaj, *Genocide*, 2023, ink on paper

[redacted]

Watching War

Marlies De Munck

A while ago I saw the film *Wil* by Belgian director Tim Mielants. The story offers a glimpse into daily life in Antwerp under Nazi occupation. I soon felt the urge to look away. The images showed me a reality that I did not want to imagine, such as that of the Jewish child who is hastily placed with the downstairs neighbours to escape deportation. Not long after, the child is sent back up the stairs by the same neighbours, only to be eventually taken captive by an aggressive *Feldgendarm*. As a viewer, as a mother, I could not bear this scene. And then the truly horrific images still had to follow, in which the persecution of the Jews and all the violence that went with it are shown with little embellishment. Although I did not know exactly with whom, I was angry that these images were shown to me. It felt as if I was being personally violated by being forced to watch this. It made me think of the scene in Stanley Kubrick's *A Clockwork Orange* where the main character is brainwashed by watching gruesome images with his eyes forced wide open. Seeing images of violence triggers a deep-seated disgust that is akin to seeing violence directly.

During the last two years, I have often felt that same visceral reaction when confronted with the horrific images from Gaza. Not only the explicit images of violence but also the vulgar displays of power, the humiliations, the destruction, even the seemingly peaceful face of a murdered child: seeing these images triggers a physical reaction in me, making me want to turn my head away. Yet I feel that I have to keep looking, although I sometimes have to force myself to do so, because not looking feels like I am doing the depicted victims an injustice. For example, I saw a photo in the newspaper of a toddler wrapped in a white sheet, her name written in hasty Arabic letters on her cheek. A second photo showed a prisoner in the West Bank with the number seventeen written on his forehead. The images reminded me of a campaign by the Dossin Kazerne in the Belgian city of Mechelen. Under the heading 'Every name counts', 25,843 names were read of the people who were deported from there to German concentration camps during the Second World War. In making their names sound out loud in the public space lies a recognition of the persons they once were and of the injustice done to them. This way, they are symbolically getting back a tiny piece of the existence that was unlawfully taken from them.

Did those two photos of Palestinian victims in the newspaper do the same thing? Is that why I feel that I have to keep looking? Surely, by showing the world how individuals are reduced to a number, how their bodies are marked like cattle for slaughter, these pictures bore witness to the ongoing dehumanization. They made the problem of their anonymity tangible. But did these images also make the dehumanized victims visible, or did they just fuel their dehumanization even further? After all, I did not know these people's names, what their individual life stories were, or what exactly had happened to them. They remained for me yet another Palestinian victim in yet another photo. Didn't these photographs, however well-intentioned, reduce them to visual material in an ongoing spectacle of violence? And to what extent, then, did these pictures truly acknowledge the real injustice done to them?

Still, hope persists that war photography can make a difference. For example, in 2025 the prestigious World Press Photo of the Year award was presented to Palestinian photographer Samar Abu Elouf. The winning photo is a poignant portrait of a nine-year-old boy from Gaza named Mahmoud, who lost both his arms in an Israeli attack. 'It's a quiet photo that tells a loud story,' said Joumana El Zein Khoury, the CEO of World Press Photo. 'It tells the story of one boy, but also of a war that will have an impact for generations.' She emphasized her belief that capturing such images can help viewers understand what's happening and inspire them to do something about it. It's a hopeful message, but does it really work? How many people continue to look at these images? And what is the effect?

The Intersection of Ethics and Aesthetics

These are the familiar questions that keep coming back about war photography: Is it good to show the horror? Is it good to look? These questions can be understood in at least two ways. First, there is the ethical dimension of looking at gruesome images: Is there anything to be gained morally? And if so,

[redacted]

for whom exactly? For the viewer or for the person depicted? Then there is the question of the political potential of war photography: What impact does it have on the violence? Can it stop the horror or prevent future violence?

To start with the first, it is intuitively plausible that witnessing violence has a moral impact on a viewer. The visceral reaction of disgust certainly seems to be a strong incentive to avoid violence, and could therefore help to raise moral awareness. This was shown by the famous Milgram experiments. In 1961, three months after the start of the trial against Nazi criminal Adolf Eichmann, psychologist Stanley Milgram investigated the extent to which people are prepared to administer painful electroshocks to fellow human beings under the influence of an authority figure. The shocking result, that an overwhelming majority of people are prepared to resort to life-threatening violence in such circumstances, provided an explanation, according to Milgram, for the large number of Germans who had participated in the Holocaust. The research result particularly supported Hannah Arendt's hypothesis that a bureaucratic delegation of power makes it easier to persuade people to do evil, because it seems to remove the personal responsibility of the individual agent.

Crucial to Milgram's experiment, however, was that the subjects did not see their victims while the electric shocks were being administered. In several later set-ups of the experiment, it turned out that the proximity between perpetrator and victim had a clear effect on the moral willingness of the subjects to continue administering the shocks. Their empathy decreased as the distance to the victim increased. Although the ethics of Milgram's method has been severely criticized by some, what can be clearly deduced from the results is that visibility and a sense of proximity have a great influence on the human moral reflex.

The same insight in the workings of the human psyche could underlie the much-discussed statements of Israeli author David Grossman, when on 12 October 2023, he branded the Hamas attack on Israeli citizens as a greater moral evil than the fifty-six years [sic] of Israeli occupation that preceded it. 'The occupation is a crime', he claimed, 'but to shoot hundreds of civilians—children and parents, elderly and sick in cold blood—that is a worse crime'. His reasoning seems to revolve around the cold-blooded nature of the violence, and it is precisely here that the intersection of the moral and the aesthetic lies. Acting 'in cold blood' requires not only the elimination of one's ethical sensibility but also of one's aesthetic capacities, as one must disregard the sensory perception of the victim's proximity. It led Grossman to say that there are gradations in the immorality of violence: 'Even in the hierarchy of evil, there is a "ranking". There is a scale of severity that common sense and natural instincts can identify. And when you see the killing fields of the music festival site, when you see Hamas terrorists on motorcycles chasing young partiers, some of whom are still dancing without realizing what's going on...'

In his moral assessment of the violence, Grossman seems to base himself primarily on the high visibility of the Israeli victims, both for the many spectators who saw the images on television and other media channels and for the Hamas fighters who committed the violence. What he implies is that it takes more murderous intent for a perpetrator to commit violence against a victim who is visible than against a victim who remains out of sight. From this psychological point of view, pressing a launch button, flying a drone or deciding in a meeting to keep borders closed to humanitarian aid would therefore be experienced as less immoral by a perpetrator, especially when operating under the authority of a superior. Accordingly, the hand-to-hand nature of Hamas' murderous acts was effectively used by many to label them as beasts. Israel's high-tech bombings were, according to the same logic, labelled 'civilized violence'.

Still, however well Grossman's reasoning can be explained psychologically, the horrific images of war victims in Gaza reveal the error in his moral classification of the violence. Because the more images the world saw, the harder it became to continue to claim that one violence was 'evidently' more immoral than another. It is precisely here that the first moral importance of showing the horrors of war becomes apparent. The constant visibility, via all kinds of media channels, gives the raw physical and psychological suffering of the civilian population a

[redacted]

greater psychological proximity, which places it alongside the videos of Hamas' violence against Israeli civilians. The proximity of the suffering pulls the crimes to the same level of immorality, because no one can claim that they could not see it.

One could argue that, as the visual documentation of the Israeli violence increased, it also became increasingly immoral, as did the global complicity of all bystanders who did not intervene. For this very reason, many pro-Israeli politicians lend their voices only to the suffering of the Jewish victims. By using their power to influence the representation of the war and by banning and even criminalizing visible protests, they deliberately try to undermine the sense of proximity to the victims, and thus also the sense of moral involvement of the population. However, with such censorship measures, these politicians do indicate that they understand the moral relevance of visibility, as they imply that visual and narrative representation can indeed have an effect on the political engagement of citizens.

The Limits of War Photography

Nevertheless, in recent decades many reasons have been formulated to question or at least problematize the moral and political effectiveness of photographic images. Susan Sontag, for example, saw a moral problem emerging in the practice of photography itself, because it presupposes a certain passivity with regard to the photographed reality. In her book *On Photography* (1977) she formulated a critique of the essentially voyeuristic character of photography for this reason, in which a reciprocal interaction with reality is replaced by the one-sided intervention of recording it. According to Sontag, this creates a morally problematic relationship to reality, especially in the case of war photography:

> *Photographing is essentially an act of non-intervention. Part of the horror of such memorable coups of contemporary photojournalism as the pictures of a Vietnamese bonze reaching for the gasoline can, of a Bengali guerrilla in the act of bayoneting a trussed-up collaborator, comes from the awareness of how plausible it has become, in situations where the photographer has the*

choice between a photograph and a life, to choose the photograph. The person who intervenes cannot record; the person who is recording cannot intervene.[1]

Sontag's critique shows that even when suffering and horror are fully visible, the viewer's moral involvement is often not sufficiently stimulated to intervene in the violence. In fact, while a photographer may be morally motivated to document injustice, direct intervention is discouraged rather than encouraged by the technical nature of photography. The camera replaces active resistance to violence by semi-passive resistance: the reproduction of the violence as an image.

In her later essay on photography, *Regarding the Pain of Others* (2003), Sontag explicitly asked whether images of war can incite political change. More than twenty-five years after she published her first essays on photography, in this later text she seems to have completely lost her faith in the political potential of photographic images. Yet she opens it with a reference to Virginia Woolf, who in 1938 expressed her belief that the shock of gruesome images of war cannot fail to unite people of good will to try to prevent war. According to Woolf, such photographs not only shake people awake, they also help the imagination to keep a reality in mind and thus to feel empathy for the victims. That empathy would then lead to resistance to subsequent wars.

Sontag herself is much more sceptical. In her view, showing horrific images of victims has never prevented another war. However much we may feel morally involved, we have become too accustomed to images of war to experience a real shock when seeing them. However gruesome, the feeling of revelation has disappeared. No unknown reality is revealed, everything is known. According to Sontag, this is also because the feeling of objectivity has disappeared that was initially still linked to the mechanical nature of photography, which, as the first fully mechanical reproduction medium ever, promised to circumvent the manipulation of human intervention. The light that falls into the camera lens would be recorded on the film in the most objective-empirical way. In this, it seemed, photography would

[redacted]

distinguish itself from drawing and painting, but also from literary or journalistic description. In *On Photography*, Sontag had already described that naive faith in photographs as an unmediated representation of reality: 'Photographed images do not seem to be statements about the world so much as pieces of it, miniatures of reality that anyone can make or acquire.'[2]

In *Regarding the Pain of Others*, Sontag pointed out that this naive belief had gradually disappeared in the twentieth century. The fact that an image is a photograph and not a painting no longer serves as irrefutable proof of the image's veracity. Today we know all too well that photos manipulate, that they can even lie. Photographers select their subject, choose a specific frame, look for the most dramatic angle, and you can never be completely sure that what you see is not staged. Even if you as a viewer are convinced that it is a faithful representation of reality, the fact that photographic images can be manipulated—if only because much more is always not shown than is shown—is enough for political opponents to question their validity as a source of evidence.

In her consideration of the value of photographic representation, Sontag seems to build on Walter Benjamin's famous thesis on the technical nature of photography. He believed that the mechanical reproduction process would reduce the sensitivity of viewers to notions such as authenticity and uniqueness when appreciating images. Whereas the aura of a traditional work of art can largely be reduced to its relic value, partly due to the assumed original physical proximity between the work, the maker, and the model, photography seems by definition to have less auratic potential. In principle, an infinite number of identical prints can be made from one and the same photo, without any relevant value distinction between original and copy. From that moment on, the cult value of a work of art inevitably gave way to its exhibition value. Wide distribution and great accessibility became the new criteria for judging the moral and political potential of an image.

Sontag continues this reasoning by assuming that the original, naive mode of reception of photographic images was still partly inspired by a desire for 'real' contact with the depicted reality. Certain photographs, which she calls 'emblems of suffering', such as the snapshot of a little boy in the Warsaw Ghetto in 1943, can be used as a memento mori—as 'secular icons', as Sontag calls them. Yet, she immediately remarks that our modern society no longer provides the sacred or meditative space that is needed to truly look at photographs in that sacralized way. So, inevitably the atavistic reflex gradually made way for a new relationship to the image, which Benjamin indicated with the term *Zerstreuung*: distracted attention. The sheer number of photographs that were distributed in the course of the twentieth century indeed made it impossible to devote the same prolonged, concentrated attention to each image. Instead, Benjamin foresaw that viewers would develop a new, lighthearted attitude, in which the gaze can jump smoothly from one image to the next.

Benjamin, in the 1930s, regarded this new way of distracted viewing as a form of emancipation: viewers could finally free themselves from the auratic spell of the image. Moreover, the much broader reach of mechanically reproduced images would democratize the aesthetic experience and therefore have revolutionary potential. Sontag, however, believed seventy years later that the constant exposure to pictures had mainly led to numbing the spectator. The frequent confrontation with images that try to attract the viewer's attention at all costs has led to the viewer becoming more indifferent to what is shown. The result is an inflation of meaning. It is simply not feasible, practically and emotionally, to let yourself be completely knocked down by every gruesome photo. In this sense, distracted viewing is not only the result of the democratization of images and therefore an expression of political emancipation but also a form of emotional self-protection.

In 2025, more than twenty years after Sontag's last essay, this evolution has only accelerated. Modern viewers are overwhelmed by digital images and are forced to divide their scarce time and attention tactically. The spontaneous aversion to gruesome pictures may play a rather negative role in this. Today, the average scrolling viewer would rather lose themselves in pleasant, aesthetic images that offer a blissful immersive experi-

[redacted]

ence than be repelled by shocking horror. Hypes such as ASMR and beauty filters on social media show how strong that desire is for satisfying experiences and feel-good photography.

All in all, Sontag not only had good arguments but also many accurate factual observations about contemporary viewing habits for being sceptical about the political potential of war photography. Simply looking at the pain of others, without further framing, is neither uplifting nor politically effective. On the contrary, it risks numbing people and making them less sensitive to the political and moral problem of war. And there is yet another problem, which was raised by Judith Butler in their book *Frames of War: When Is Life Grievable?* (2009). Although they agree with Sontag's criticism that photographic images are never a neutral representation of reality, Butler believes that Sontag still paid too little attention to the bigger picture. Not only the way an image is framed by the photographer but also the cultural framework in which we do or do not see images and within which people can or cannot appear as victims influences the political impact of war photography. Who and what may be depicted, and how it is framed, is decided at a higher level, or is even unconsciously part of the dominant culture. Whose life is seen as grievable is therefore not simply a matter of individual sensitivity to an image.

That Israel has now killed more journalists in Gaza than were killed in the American Civil War, the First and Second World Wars, the Korean War, the Vietnam War (including Cambodia and Laos), the wars in Yugoslavia in the 1990s and 2000s, and the post-9/11 war in Afghanistan combined, is of course no insignificant fact in this regard. In order to control the constant stream of images, draconian measures are needed, with international media completely denied access to the war zone and nearly two hundred local journalists murdered (and still counting). Although, as already suggested above, such attempts to control the larger framework mainly signal a belief in and fear of the political effects of visual and journalistic representation, the strategy of large-scale framing of the Palestinians as terrorists and anti-Semites seems to be working. During the first year and a half of the war on Gaza, official Western imagery and reporting consistently confirmed the same, supposedly neutral ideological framework that, not coincidentally, also reflects the political position of most Western countries. The conflict was presented as 'complex' and therefore impossible to judge, and the one-sided siege of Gaza was consistently presented as a symmetrical 'war' between two warring parties. In this way, both Sontag and Butler seem to be right in their scepticism about the political power of war photography. Even if the gruesome images did reach the Western media, they did not have the clout to change the political course because of the larger ideological framing in which the Palestinian victims appeared as mere collateral damage, not as deliberately murdered human beings.

Haunting Images

Yet we must ask ourselves where such defeatism ultimately leads—if only because the discourse of Sontag and Butler also creates an intellectual framework within which things can or cannot appear. Hope, for example, becomes very difficult to imagine and represent when images are considered impotent by definition. Moreover, we must ask ourselves whether there is actually a valid alternative to showing violence. Even if people look away, even if they do not use their voices to protest and denounce the violence, there still seem to be many reasons to continue showing images of war. These reasons are also both moral and political-practical in nature.

To begin with, I noticed over the last year that I started to experience new forms of empathy through the online stream of images that reached me directly from Gaza via social media. A kind of shortcut seems to have emerged here that can bypass the dominant narrative of the official media channels. On Facebook, I follow the messages from Gaza Soup Kitchen, an initiative of a family in Northern Gaza who, through fundraising, have managed to prepare hot meals for their local community every day for more than a year and a half now. They document their enterprise in a continuous stream of photos and videos. 'We believe in transparency through visual storytelling,' is the slogan on their website. Despite all my critical

[redacted]

awareness of the potentially misleading nature of photographic images, this kind of visual storytelling still has a clear moral impact on me. The images stick. As a viewer, I am concerned about the joys and sorrows of these people. I follow the daily updates to know how they are doing. Of course, that is exactly the emotional effect that is aimed for. The machinery of the Gaza Soup Kitchen is driven by altruism, but at least as much by pragmatism. Ultimately, money has to come in to save people from famine. Behind the scenes, from Washington DC, one of the brothers of the family keeps the business going: the fundraising, the online photo reporting, the financial transfers and the logistical organization for the distribution of money, food, water, clothing, medicine, education.

The images are very 'Instagrammable': beautiful children looking straight into the camera, the colours of their outfits digitally pimped (I presume); there is close-up, cookbook-style food photography, large steaming cooking pots doused with handfuls of colourful herbs, beautifully arranged dishes, an ever-smiling team of chefs who work tirelessly for their fellow citizens; and then there is the irresistibly cute toddler Hamoudi with his sweet eyes and fluffy kittens. You could almost forget that it is war photography, if it were not for the total destruction that remains visible in the background. The bright, cheerful colours contrast sharply with the pale grey and brown of the dust and rubble, of the ash and smoke from the continuous bombardments. Every now and then the suffering is shown a little more prominently, but it is never bloody. The photos are always accompanied by snappy commentary, written in a recognizable online idiom, such as this one: 'Our crew at the frontlines of hunger today in Al Zawaydah went through 450 pounds of zucchinis to boost the nutritional value of meals, adding freshness to the lentils and pasta.' In the photo, the bright yellow-green of the courgettes contrasts nicely with the dark mixture of herbs.

What I see here is aesthetics in action. Victims who are not only beautiful but also visually clever. They know how to harness the viewer's desire for authenticity. The promise of transparency with regard to the donors is fulfilled by the many personal stories and the detailed descriptions of recipes and ingredients. This is scroll material—not doomscrolling, but next-level war photography. I want to see more of it, post after post, reel after reel, immersed in the colourful, dramatic world of the Gaza Soup Kitchen. Still, any contemporary image digester knows well enough that this kind of image belongs to the realm of appearances. Sontag's critique certainly applies here; the spectator is emotionally manipulated. But it happens by enchantment, rather than by shock. While viewing, I feel deep admiration for the ability to keep seeking out beauty and laughter in such harsh circumstances, and for the courage of the Gaza Soup Kitchen to keep going. The most important moral effect, however, comes from the sharp contrast: the more beautiful the laughing people in the images, the more haunting they become. I am well aware that their laughter drowns out the most harrowing reality.

Nevertheless, these pictures give me hope. Of course, like all war photography, they need a narrative and a framework that indicates how to interpret them. But this is not just about passing on information. Without the photographs, with only storylines, the fundraising would undoubtedly not work as well as it does. This is a fact of war photography that Sontag also recognizes, even though, on its own, it cannot guarantee an accurate interpretation. 'Harrowing photographs do not inevitably lose their power to shock,' she claims, continuing that 'they are not much help if the task is to understand. Narratives can make us understand. Photographs do something else: they haunt us.'[3]

In the same way, the photographs of the Gaza Soup Kitchen haunt the viewer like an 'always absent-presence,' as Jacques Derrida described it in his hauntology. While documenting the absence of normal life, they simultaneously create an experience of permanent proximity. Their specific aura allows no distance to what is seen. This turns the haunted viewer into an eyewitness who becomes morally involved.

In her earlier text on photography, Sontag also mentioned the testimonial potential of photographic images, but she did not relate this to their haunting 'absent-present' character. Instead, she connected it to the mechanical nature of photography as evidence for the true existence of what it depicts:

Photographs furnish evidence. Something we hear about, but doubt, seems proven when we're shown a photograph of it. [...] A photograph passes for incontrovertible proof that a given thing happened. The picture may distort; but there is always a presumption that something exists, or did exist, which is like what's in the picture. [...] Virtuosi of the noble image like Alfred Stieglitz and Paul Strand, composing mighty, unforgettable photographs decade after decade, still want, first of all, to show something 'out there'.[4]

Knowing that something is happening 'out there' is the beginning of political awareness, and therefore of the emancipation of the viewer. It is the condition for political engagement that can lead to intervention, or at least to perpetrators being held accountable. Here we find yet another political aspect of war photography. A good example is the drama of the murdered ambulance workers in Gaza, known as the Rafah paramedic massacre in March 2025. The aid workers were 'out there', on their way to save victims, but no one could or wanted to testify about how they had met their end. Only because there was camera footage could this massacre be recognized and acknowledged as a war crime. This incident shows how much photography, despite all legitimate concerns about manipulation and framing, can have a direct political impact.

Finally, the capacity of war photography to bear witness also encompasses an existential dimension, the effect of which has more long-term political consequences. This is the simple fact that looking is also 'facing'. Seeing something is the first and indispensable step towards recognizing a reality. In this way, a photographic image, thanks to its capacity to bear witness, can transform into an icon of authenticity. The photograph tells: someone once saw this. One day it will be seen by other eyes. By being seen, something has dug itself deeper into the structure of existence; it can never not have been there again. This existential dimension of war photography not only has an emancipating effect on the viewer but also—and above all—on the one who is seen. It was precisely this that Palestinian war photographer Fatima Hassouna referred to when she stated:

'I want a death that the world will hear, an impact that will remain through time, and a timeless image that cannot be buried by time or place.' She received that loud death on 16 April 2025. A few weeks later, during the opening ceremony of the Cannes Film Festival, French actress and head of the jury Juliette Binoche paid tribute to Hassouna in full view of the cameras. The open letter from more than 350 film stars, published at the same time, ends tellingly with the following lines: 'For Fatma, for all those who die in indifference. Cinema has a duty to carry their messages, to reflect our societies.' Photographic reflection, then, becomes a moral duty.

It is safe to conclude that Sontag formulated her question too categorically. Of course, violence will never be completely eradicated, and war can never be completely prevented, certainly not by photography alone. But there exist many more nuanced positions between moral perfection and defeatism. Today we see that finally a shift is beginning to take place in public opinion about Gaza, and even in Western politics. That this has everything to do with the horrific images that keep haunting us, despite the dominant Western frameworks, is evident from the words with which Belgian Prime Minister Bart De Wever heralded this change. Although he had been ardently defending Israel's war strategy for over a year and a half, he suddenly declared at a press conference that the images from Gaza were 'unbearable to look at'. Other European leaders made similar statements, always referring to the images of the atrocities and the victims of the violence. Whether this will eventually lead to change in their political actions remains to be seen. But at least it seems clear that there would have been no change of course at all if we had not seen all those haunting pictures of the war.

Notes

1 • Susan Sontag, *On Photography* (New York: RosettaBooks, 2005), p. 8.
2 • Ibid., p. 2.
3 • Susan Sontag, *Regarding the Pain of Others* (London: Penguin Books, 2003), p. 78.
4 • Sontag, *On Photography*, p. 3.

References

- Benjamin, Walter. 'The Work of Art in the Age of Mechanical Reproduction'. In *Illuminations*, ed. Hannah Arendt, trans. Harry Zohn, from the 1935 essay. New York: Schocken Books, 1969.
- Butler, Judith. *Frames of War: When Is Life Grievable?* New York: Verso, 2009.
- Derrida, Jacques. *Specters of Marx: The State of the Debt, the Work of Mourning, and the New International.* London: Routledge, 1994.
- Ellis-Petersen, Hannah. '"If I die, I want a loud death": Gaza photojournalist killed by Israeli airstrike'. *The Guardian*, 18 April 2025.
- Gaza Soup Kitchen, www.gazasoupkitchen.com.
- Grossman, David. 'Who will we be when we rise from the ashes?', *The Times of Israel*, 20 October 2023.
- Kubrick, Stanley. *A Clockwork Orange.* Film. Hawk Films, 1971.
- Mielants, Tim. *Wil.* Film. 2023.
- Milgram, Stanley. *Obedience to Authority: An Experimental View.* New York: Harper & Row, 1974.
- Sontag, Susan. *On Photography.* New York: RosettaBooks, 2005. Originally published in 1977.
- Sontag, Susan. *Regarding the Pain of Others.* London: Penguin Books, 2003.

[redacted]

Bearing Witness
The Ethics of Seeing in Humanitarian Photography

Interview with Julie David de Lossy, Bruno De Cock (Médecins Sans Frontières)

Marlies De Munck
Pascal Gielen

What can an image do? The question lingers like an after-image on the retina, pulsing in the space between engagement and indifference. The power of photography in conflict zones has long been debated. Does it make distant suffering tangible, or does it reduce human lives to mere spectacle? Does it mobilize solidarity, or does it risk numbing its audience through endless repetition?

Médecins Sans Frontières (MSF) has weighed these questions for decades. As a humanitarian medical care organization operating on the frontlines of war, displacement, and disaster, its work is necessarily entangled with the politics of visibility. The stories MSF tells through its images, and just as importantly, the ones it chooses not to show, help shape how we understand global crises. They often determine whether a war remains an abstraction or enters our living rooms as a moral imperative.

This is why Julie David de Lossy and Bruno De Cock—two professionals at the heart of MSF's visual strategy—are crucial voices in this book. Julie, as MSF's Multimedia Team Leader, guides audiovisual producers (photographers, videographers) on how best to document crises without exploiting suffering. Her background in photojournalism and conflict prevention NGOs informs an approach that seeks to preserve both truth and dignity. Bruno, as Audiovisual Senior Advisor and Media Database Manager, curates and safeguards MSF's visual archive, ensuring that the images used in advocacy and communication align with the organization's ethical principles while moving the thinking of photography within MSF forward. Together, they offer a rare insight into the ethics of humanitarian photography—the dilemmas of representation, the fine line between witness and voyeur, and the responsibilities that come with framing a world in crisis.

Let's begin with an open question: What should images do? Both personally and professionally, what do you believe photographs of conflict, war, and crises should achieve? Susan Sontag, in Regarding the Pain of Others, *argues that war photography does not necessarily lead to political change but can also desensitize viewers. She questions whether repeated exposure to suffering actually incites solidarity, or if it instead causes disengagement. Do you think humanitarian photography can still have an impact, or do we risk numbing audiences with too many images of crisis?*

Julie David de Lossy • I think images still have the power to create connection. They should bridge the distance between those suffering and those who might act in solidarity. But they should also resist becoming just another shocking spectacle—something we consume and then forget. The challenge is to ensure that images don't just evoke pity, but foster a deeper understanding.

Bruno De Cock • Within MSF, our images must inform, bear witness, and ultimately protect. We are not neutral observers; we are part of the humanitarian landscape. That comes with responsibility. Images need to respect the dignity of those depicted and avoid exploitation. The challenge is: How do we keep people engaged without relying on predictable visual language?

JDdL • Another crucial element is avoiding the reinforcement of existing narratives. Too often, media representations reduce war and suffering to either statistics or spectacle. Our role is to introduce nuance, to bring in voices and perspectives that might otherwise remain unheard and unseen.

BDC • Exactly. And that's where the role of the photographer becomes crucial. Who is behind the lens matters. We've seen that when local photographers document their own communities, the resulting images are very different from those taken by outsiders. The framing, the choice of subjects, the way people are portrayed—it all changes. It's something we're actively working on: shifting the visual narrative by ensuring that the people we photograph are not just subjects, but participants in how they are represented.

JDdL • And this extends beyond just the photographer's identity. It's also about how the image is taken. We try to create space for agency, allowing individuals to decide how they want to be portrayed. For example, when covering mental healthcare for migrants, we've worked with photographers who engage in a dialogue with the people they photograph. This changes the dynamic—instead of being passive subjects, people assert their presence.

BDC • Another strategy is thinking about how we frame images. Some of the most powerful images we've received were taken by refugees themselves in Calais, using disposable cameras. The resulting photos were not polished, but they carried an undeniable rawness and authenticity. These were not pictures taken about refugees; they were taken by them. The perspective shifts entirely.

When looking at MSF's image archive—malnourished children, emergency medical procedures—do you feel these images still provoke empathy? Or are they at risk of becoming part of a repetitive visual language?

JDdL • This is something we reflect on constantly. We know that repeated exposure to suffering can lead to desensitization. But at the same time, these crises are ongoing—people are still suffering. If we stop showing it, we risk making it invisible.

BDC • One way we try to counteract that is by embedding images within personal testimonies. A single image detached from its context can become another tragic, passive portrayal. But when it's paired with a voice—when the story is about the person, not just their suffering—we shift the frame.

JDdL • Exactly. It's not just about what you show, but how you show it. We've also noticed how engagement changes, depending on the framing of an image. For example, when we work with local photographers who understand the community, the resulting images resonate differently. They capture details an outsider might miss—the body language, the subtle expressions of resilience, the small yet profound moments of dignity.

BDC • We also see how fatigue plays a role. If we look at Gaza, for example, people have seen so many war images that they start filtering them out. But when individuals share personal images, with direct messages like, 'This is my home, destroyed', it seems to break through that indifference. The challenge is figuring out how to apply that lesson in a broader humanitarian context.

MSF presents itself as a neutral humanitarian actor. But if your images serve advocacy, if they speak out against injustice, isn't that already taking a political stance?

JDdL • This is a constant discussion within MSF. We do not engage in activism in the sense of taking sides in conflicts, but we do speak out. We report what we see: people dying because they lack medical access, bombed hospitals, epidemics that could have been prevented. That's not political in the partisan sense, but it does challenge power structures.

BDC • We have to be extremely careful with language. In Sudan, for example, we operate in areas controlled by different factions. If we frame our messaging incorrectly, we risk being denied access—or worse, endangering our teams. So, yes, we are neutral in the sense that we treat everyone, but we are not silent.

Speaking of storytelling, many MSF images are strikingly beautiful—carefully composed, with attention to colour and light. This calls to mind

[redacted]

what Jacques Rancière argues in his work on aesthetics and politics: that art does not simply represent *reality but actively* reconfigures *the way we see it. He speaks of the 'redistribution of the sensible'—how certain images, voices, and perspectives are made visible while others remain excluded. In that sense, visual testimony itself can be a political act, particularly when it challenges dominant visual narratives. Do you think humanitarian photography, when done consciously, can function in this way? Or do you worry that aestheticization risks softening the reality of crisis?*

JDdL • It's a paradox. Beauty draws people in. It makes them pause. But we must ensure that beauty doesn't dilute the urgency of suffering. In some cases, beauty can even reinforce the impact of an image. When we worked with a photographer in Lebanon covering mental healthcare for migrants, the patients were not just depicted as victims but as individuals asserting their presence. One woman, for instance, chose to be photographed in a way that communicated her own strength, looking directly into the camera, not broken but resilient.

BDC • Another aspect of aesthetics is intentionality. When we select photographers, we do so not just for their technical skills but for their ability to see beyond clichés. It's about avoiding the 'expected' image and searching for something different. Sometimes that means consciously challenging mainstream visual narratives. We also see how certain aesthetic decisions influence the reception of images. For example, the already mentioned black-and-white images taken by refugees in Calais look entirely different from what a professional photographer would produce. These images aren't staged, and their rawness conveys authenticity in a way that we, as outsiders, could never replicate. They show a reality that is both personal and political.

In today's polarized climate, humanitarian organizations like MSF often find themselves caught between conflicting political interests, between far right and woke, where neutrality is often seen as a moral failure, or even as a political stance in itself. How do you navigate these tensions?

BDC • The migration issue is a perfect example. Some politicians call us a 'taxi service' for saving lives at sea. But what's the alternative? Letting people drown? And yet, within activist circles, we sometimes get criticized for not taking a stronger stance against European border policies. We're always walking a tightrope.

We've spoken about the power of images, their ethical dilemmas, and their political implications. But perhaps a good closing question is: Why do you continue to do this work? Despite all the challenges, what keeps you engaged?

JDdL • What keeps me going is seeing how images can shift perception. When people say, 'I had no idea this was happening', that means photography is still doing its job. It's about documenting, but also about creating a response, even if that response is small. If someone donates, writes to their government, or simply cares—that's already something.

BDC • For me, it's about the responsibility of witnessing. If we don't document what we see, does it even exist beyond the people experiencing it? Certain crises become invisible because they are not 'newsworthy' enough. Some places, people, and types of suffering get more attention than others. We try to counter that by telling the stories that might otherwise be ignored.

JDdL • And it's also about trust. We are given access to people's most vulnerable moments, which means we carry their stories with us. That's not something I take lightly. If we choose to show an image, we need to ensure it does justice to the person in it.

BDC • Ultimately, it's about integrity. We can't control how every image is received or used, but we can control

[redacted]

why we take them and how we tell the story. As long as we remain honest in that, I think the work remains worth doing.

[redacted]

Measures Against Violence
Theatre in Unsettled Times

Erwin Jans

When Mr. Keuner, the thinker, spoke out against violence before a crowded audience, he noticed the people backing away and leaving. He turned around—and behind him stood Violence.

'What did you just say?' asked Violence.

'I was speaking in favour of violence,' replied Mr. Keuner.

Later, when Mr. Keuner had gone, his students asked him about his backbone. Mr. Keuner answered, 'I have no backbone to be shattered. It is I who must outlive violence.'

And then Mr. Keuner told the following story:

Once, during a time of illegality, a police officer entered the home of Mr. Egge, a man who had learned to say no. The officer presented him with an order issued by those in control of the city, stating that every home he entered would henceforth belong to him, along with any food he demanded, and that every man he encountered must serve him.

The officer sat down in a chair, demanded food, washed himself, lay down, and asked—facing the wall before falling asleep—'Will you serve me?'

Mr. Egge covered him with a blanket, swatted the flies away, stood guard over his sleep, and for seven years did as he was told. But in all those years, there was one thing he carefully avoided: speaking. And when the seven years had passed, and the officer had grown fat on food, sleep, and commands, he died. Mr. Egge wrapped him in the soiled blanket, dragged him out of the house, cleaned the bedding, whitewashed the walls, breathed freely once more, and answered: 'No.'

'What Did You Just Say?'

Mr. Keuner is a fictional character conceived in the mid-1920s by German playwright and writer Bertolt Brecht (1898–1956), who continued to write short prose around him until his death. *Measures Against Violence* is among the most well-known. Brecht penned most of these stories during the precarious democratic experiment of the Weimar Republic and the rise of Nazism in Germany—a development that forced Brecht into exile from 1933 to 1948. The name 'Keuner' (pronounced 'koiner') is said to echo the Swabian dialect for *keiner*, meaning 'nobody'. Mr. Keuner is thus Mr. Nobody. It might also be a reference to the Greek word koinos, meaning 'common' or 'public good'. Mr. Keuner is both everyone and no one. Perhaps his name also faintly echoes the tale in *The Odyssey*, where Odysseus escapes the grip of the Cyclops by calling himself 'Nobody'. 'Who did this?'—'Nobody did it!'

Without drawing oversimplified parallels between then and now, one cannot help but detect something of our current condition in the political crisis that Brecht faced. Both Mr. Keuner's story and that of Mr. Egge—which Keuner uses to explain his behaviour—speak of survival under the shadow of grave threat. Violence suddenly looms behind Mr. Keuner. Who or what this Violence is remains unspecified, and that vagueness only adds to the terror—it catches you from behind, unseen. The moment is clearly urgent. A response is needed.

At first glance, both Mr. Keuner and Mr. Egge seem to lack courage, even backbone. They are not resistance heroes in the romanticized mould: principled, forceful, unbending. And yet, Brecht's fable calls for a more attentive reading.

Is Mr. Keuner merely a coward because he speaks against violence and then immediately reverses course when confronted by it? Is this the opposite of 'speaking truth to power', the ideal we often ascribe to the independent thinker? Or is he, like Mr. Egge, a strategist—waiting for the right moment to say no? Their resistance is neither frontal nor direct, neither activist nor public. Both seem to reject heroism and martyrdom, grand gestures and lofty words. Brecht was too keenly aware of the crushing weight of real conditions—of violence—to churn out cardboard heroes fit for a Hollywood script. His (anti-)heroes, even in his plays, attempt to manoeuvre within their circumstances. They are not conformists, but neither are they passive.

Mr. Keuner knows precisely what violence can do to him—it can shatter his spine. And he knows that he, the thinking one, is more essential than violence itself. He must survive. Mr. Egge obeys the officer, but avoids the ultimate submission: he never says yes. He refuses consent. Egge has learned not only to say no, but to say it at the right moment. Waiting, or biding one's time—making use of duration and the long arc—

[redacted]

becomes a form of resistance, or at the very least a strategy.

Curiously, Mr. Keuner explains his stance by telling another story. Fiction explains fiction. A story is always a detour, a postponement, a ruse, a lie, a protection, a form of distance, a different vantage point—a space to think before deciding. Before saying no, perhaps at the right time?

We live in dark times—*in finsteren Zeiten*, as Brecht wrote in his famous poem 'To Those Who Follow in Our Wake'. The desire is great among artists and theatre-makers—those who literally have a stage—to speak out on the urgent matters of our time: the accelerating ecological crisis, the rapid shift to the right in politics, the concept of gender fluidity, the necessity of postcolonial thinking, the importance of inclusivity, the growing democratic deficit, and more. The pressure to do so with ever more clarity and explicitness continues to mount, leaving less and less space for nuance.

In our hyper-polarized world, the opposing camps demand more fervently than ever that those who speak must also justify themselves. *What did you just say?*—that question now takes the form of a statement, a reproach, a threat, a demand, a form of coercion. It is the burden under which artists, though not they alone, now operate. A single ill-judged phrase, a nuance uttered at the wrong time, a term deemed incorrect... and the consequences can be severe.

On the (far) right of the political spectrum, a floodgate has burst: words and ideas long considered taboo are once again spoken aloud. Meanwhile, on the (far) left, a vocabulary of political correctness has developed—often accompanied by a cancel culture. At this moment, the war in Gaza is arguably the most linguistically charged conflict, a fault line splitting political conversations in two. Some words make all the difference. Is Israel committing genocide in Gaza? The mere use of that term can tear camps apart. Even Donald Trump now appropriates the word 'genocide'—albeit in the context of accusing South Africa of committing one against white people (!), thus threatening to drain the term of all meaning.

It is no coincidence, then, that Brecht's fable is fundamentally about language: about lying, about silence, and about escaping the labyrinth of speech itself. Who may speak about what? Who is entitled to have an opinion? Who may speak for whom? And who may use which vocabulary?

These are the very questions that the artists of Toneelhuis in Antwerp have been grappling with in recent years. Their work has frequently revolved around war and loss, grief and remembrance—especially in the past season. They staged *Mother Courage and Her Children*, Brecht's legendary play in which a mother loses her children to the very war that also sustains her livelihood. They created *The Grief of Red Granny*, an operatic and sensory exploration of African mourning rituals, and *Queen Elisabeth*, a piece about a woman whose right to grief is denied when she is barred from attending her husband's funeral. They worked on *Guernica Guernica*, a piece originally intended as a comedy titled *Viva Guernica*—a title that became untenable following the war in Ukraine and the bloodshed in Gaza. Soon, they will bring *Before the Retirement* by Thomas Bernhard to the stage—a play in which the legacy of Nazism creeps into the family living room.

Mother Courage in Kurdish

It is no accident that this reflection begins with a text by Brecht. Not only does he remain a crucial point of reference in the debate surrounding politically engaged theatre, but one of the productions I wish to discuss is *Mother Courage and Her Children*, directed by Lisaboa Houbrechts.

Mother Courage, perhaps Brecht's most iconic play, tells the story of the canteen woman Anna Fierling during the Thirty Years' War (1618–1648)—a brutal conflict between Catholics and Protestants that entangled nearly all of Europe's major powers. A canteen woman was a woman permitted to travel with the troops, selling food, drink, and daily supplies to the soldiers. Anna Fierling earns her nickname, 'Mother Courage', for fearlessly pulling her cart with fifty loaves through enemy fire. War is her livelihood. Soldiers are her clients. The fact that she eventually follows the Catholic enemy army doesn't bother her—the business must go on. But the cost of her trade is steep: she loses all three of her children. And yet, at the end of the play, she follows the troops once again.

Brecht's focus is not on portraying the horrors of war, but on the moral implications of living—and making decisions—in wartime. Influenced by Marxist thought, Brecht saw a deep connection between capitalism, fascism, and war. For him, theatre was a means to expose that entanglement. Like many opponents of Nazism, Brecht's life became nomadic after Hitler's rise to power in 1933. He moved between the capitals of Europe, found refuge in Denmark, later in Sweden, and eventually in the United States. From these various places, through plays, poems, and essays, he waged an unrelenting battle against fascism, developing his theory of epic theatre along the way. In the US, he was prosecuted for un-American activities, prompting his return in 1949 to East Berlin, where he and his wife Helene Weigel founded the Berliner Ensemble.

Mother Courage was written in 1939 during Brecht's exile in Sweden. It was intended as a warning to Scandinavia not to side with Hitler for economic reasons. Brecht wanted to instil in his audience a visceral loathing of war, and placed his hope in the emergence of a socialist order. Capitalism, he believed, had to be recognized and fought as the true engine of war.

To Brecht, Mother Courage embodied the alliance of capitalism and war, and her stance was to be condemned. Yet the character has grown far more complex than Brecht himself may have intended. In his view, her trade perpetuated the war, and even the deaths of her children failed to awaken her. But many spectators see her primarily as a victim of forces utterly beyond her control. They admire her courage and tenacity. For them, Mother Courage evokes not disgust, but compassion.

'I only feel emotion when I have a headache—never when I write, for then I think,' Brecht is said to have remarked. After his conversion to Marxism in the late 1920s, writing became, for him, a near-scientific activity; a controlled experiment devoted to clarifying social relations and transforming society by provoking deliberate, socially useful reactions in the audience. That was the goal of his *epic theatre*: to confront the spectator with evidence, so that they might draw clear and critical conclusions for themselves.

It's essential to remember that Brecht wrote in (and against) a time when an irrational, pathos-driven rhetoric—steeped in nation, race, and homeland—was seducing the masses. His now-famous strategies for distancing audience and actor from emotion and identification are well known: estrangement effects, interruptions of the action, use of song and signage, scene summaries that shift emphasis from what happens to how it happens, vast leaps in time between scenes...

The *What did you just say?* that Lisaboa Houbrechts encountered with this production touches on her relationship to Brecht's legacy of political theatre—a legacy still partly guarded by copyright law. A theatre-maker is still not free to do whatever they wish with Brecht's texts. Houbrechts' intention to radically rewrite *Mother Courage* ran up against contractual limits on the use of the original text and music. That legacy stands as the model of Brecht's epic theatre, as described above. Houbrechts enters into a headstrong dialogue with that legacy, pushing the boundaries of—and perhaps stepping beyond—of what the contracts allow.

According to the British theatre critic Martin Esslin, Brecht's major plays provoke far more than just rational societal analysis in their audiences: 'Beneath the rational, propagandistic surface there always lies a deep emotional layer—repressed, but all the more powerfully active for that very reason. This suppressed emotional content resonates with the deeper regions of the audience's mind and is perceived as poetic force. The tension between the author's conscious intention and the unconscious emotional content—unknown even to him—is, in Brecht's case, the source of his poetic strength'.

In her staging, Houbrechts taps into that emotional undercurrent and translates it into a musical and abstract-visual poetry. The stage is dominated by an immense black sphere, pushed by actors around a watery surface in a circular movement. It is a distant and abstract memory of Mother Courage's cart, but also much more. It is the ultimate feminine symbol. It is, of course, the Earth—but also history. A massive cannonball. Carrying within it all the suffering of war. In Houbrechts'

[redacted]

hands, *Mother Courage* becomes a mythical figure—like Brueghel's *Dulle Griet*, marching through the ravaged landscape of history. Death and life, destruction and fertility, bound together in a single image. Houbrechts sees Mother Courage as an ambiguous figure: both perpetrator and victim, mother and merchant.

But for Houbrechts, war is not merely something that rages between nations and peoples. It also plays out within the family, and within the intimate terrain of the female body. Courage takes her place in an impressive lineage of enigmatic female figures in Lisaboa's work: *Dulle Griet*, *Medea*, *Yerma*... She strips the Thirty Years' War of its historical concreteness: no dates, no names, no locations. What remains is the notion of a religious war between Catholics and Protestants—a prototype of every war, past and present.

Houbrechts turns her focus to the 'family'—Anna Fierling (portrayed by Lubna Azabal and Laetitia Dosch) and her three children: the brave Eilif (Aydin Isleyen), the honest Schweizerkas (Pietro Quadrino), and the traumatized but empathetic Kattrin (Lisi Estaras), who cannot speak. The story of war is told from the viewpoint of those who suffer most: the little people for whom war always rhymes with catastrophe.

Nationalism and racism are also central themes. In the play's opening scene, Mother Courage introduces her three children, each fathered by a different man on different European battlefields. Brecht intentionally creates a multinational family as a counter to Nazi racial nationalism. Houbrechts goes further: unlike Brecht's Courage, hers is not the biological mother of the children, but their adoptive mother. She is a barren woman. Her relation to femininity, sexuality, and motherhood is as complex as it is ambiguous—moving between care and pragmatism, between affection and detachment. In a newly added text, Houbrechts' Courage declares: 'I am not a woman. I'm not even a man.' The gender question is essential to her—a fundamentally political concern.

In a way, the other characters also belong to Courage's 'extended family': the cook (Koen De Sutter) and the chaplain (Joeri Happel), both of whom court her, and the sex worker

Yvette (Laura De Geest), who follows the troops. The various soldiers who appear are all played by Alain Franco. War slowly corrodes the relationships between these figures. All bonds are touched—tainted—by the conflict.

For her alienation effects, Houbrechts does not rely on Brecht's classic techniques, such as the fragmentation into episodic scenes spanning years or the deliberate interruptions of the dramatic action. Instead, her staging unfolds like a dream—or a nightmare. But she does embrace a plurality of languages and sonic registers: various forms of song, music, and sound shape the sensory world of *Mother Courage*.

That soundscape consists of three layers: the songs from the 1930s, originally composed by Paul Dessau for Brecht's production; the Kurdish vocal music of Aydin Isleyen, who plays Eilif; and an original score by Alain Franco. This musical collage brings a new temporal dimension into play—one that reaches beyond Brecht's time and speaks directly to our present. These are sound-images that conjure associations and resonances in space, allowing each listener's uniquely shaped memory to run a parallel sound-film beside Brecht's text.

Through the multinational and multicultural backgrounds of the performers, the polyphony of languages (Dutch, French, Kurdish, Hebrew), and the symbolic associations evoked by the immense black sphere, a great deal of 'world' is brought into the production. Unsurprisingly, not all spectators or Brecht purists found themselves at ease in this reinterpretation. What did you just say?—more than one devotee of Brecht must have asked after seeing the performance.

Himmler at the Kitchen Table

While Houbrechts chooses a strategy of abstraction and universality in her version of *Mother Courage*—invoking multiple languages and symbolic registers—Tom Dewispelaere of Olympique Dramatique opts for a historicizing approach in his staging of *Before the Retirement (a Comedy of the German Soul)*, a play written by Thomas Bernhard in the late 1970s. That specific era is invoked in both the set design and the costuming. Paradoxically,

[redacted]

it is precisely this anchoring in the past that makes the play feel acutely relevant today—as will soon become clear.

Bernhard's oeuvre is marked, both explicitly and implicitly, by the lingering, unresolved legacy of National Socialism, which continues to haunt Germany and Austria. In *Before the Retirement*, he portrays the annual celebration of Heinrich Himmler's birthday—October 7th—by the characters with unrestrained grotesquery. Through this provocative, even hilarious staging of far-right nostalgia for fascist and Nazi ideals, Bernhard unleashes a disturbing portrait.

The play unfolds in the claustrophobic, incestuous household of the Höller family. Rudolf Höller—once a concentration camp commandant and now a highly respected judge—is nearing retirement. For him and his sister Vera, Himmler's birthday is a sacred occasion. Their younger sister, Clara, confined to a wheelchair, stands apart from the ceremony. She bears the weight of the past and watches in dismay as her family embraces its horrors. What follows is an ideological power play drenched in guilt, resentment, denial, and moral decay—bound together by familial ties that can never quite be severed.

In *Before the Retirement*, Bernhard exposes the impotence and hypocrisy of post-war Germany (and Austria) in confronting its own Nazi past—the pervasive silence surrounding wartime guilt. Through the disturbing, far-right rhetoric of his fossilized characters, he vents his disgust. Yet at the same time, Bernhard admits: perhaps we ourselves are not so different.

The immediate reason for staging this play lies in the alarming normalization of vocabulary and ideologies that are the direct heirs of the far-right extremism of the 1930s and '40s. Statements we once thought had been relegated to the margins of political discourse have re-entered the mainstream. That which once could not be spoken, now is.

This is why the play had to be historicized. The Himmler commemoration, which in the 1970s had to take place behind closed doors, may soon, frighteningly, become part of public ritual once again. The performance wants its audience to think about this possibility—and what it means.

Guernica or Guernica?

While in Bernhard's play the question *What did you just say?* lies at the very heart of the drama, in FC Bergman's work, it emerges primarily from the context in which the performance was conceived. With *Guernica Guernica*, FC Bergman dares to pose an uncomfortable question: What do we first associate with the name 'Guernica'? The Basque town bombed in 1937 during the Spanish Civil War—with the aid of Nazi Germany—or the iconic painting Pablo Picasso made of that same bombardment? The horror, or its artistic representation?

The title *Guernica Guernica* points to this duality. And yet that was not the production's original title. Initially, it was to be called *Viva Guernica*. The performance was conceived after the Russian invasion of Ukraine, but before Hamas' attack on Israel. FC Bergman's intent was to create a wordless, satirical piece on war, inspired in part by Chaplin's *The Great Dictator*. As an internationally renowned collective, FC Bergman often works within co-productions and festival circuits, where institutional dialogue is inevitable. Early talks with co-producers and programmers were smooth and positive.

But on 7 October 2023, a new geopolitical reality emerged. The brutal, murderous attack by Hamas on Israel, which killed over a thousand people, and the massive military invasion of Gaza by Israel—resulting in tens of thousands of deaths—shifted the context dramatically. A question rose to the surface: In light of such horrors, was a satirical approach to war still legitimate? Not only co-producers and programmers asked this, but the makers themselves.

Theatre is, by its very nature, created in the *hic et nunc*. And that *here and now* is inevitably shaped by what is happening in the world at that moment. FC Bergman is not a company known for taking overt political stances. Rather, it works with ambiguity, multiplicity, and the disorienting power of imagery—offering audiences interpretive space instead of ideological instruction. For FC Bergman, their engagement lies entirely within their performances, not in declarations outside them. But even this position comes under pressure.

What did you just say? To speak out explicitly against Israel's military violence and call for a boycott—economic, military, political, academic—is, in certain contexts, immediately equated with anti-Semitism. In Germany, this is historically an especially sensitive issue. And in Trump's America, virtually any expression of solidarity with Palestinians is swiftly branded as anti-Semitic.

At the same time, international cultural festivals and major artistic institutions are now being scrutinized by pro-Palestinian activist groups. Their funding is combed through for ties to, or support for, Israel. Multiple petitions circulate from international humanitarian organizations calling for condemnation of Israeli violence and the severing of all institutional collaborations. Signing such petitions can carry serious consequences: artists may find themselves blacklisted, denied by festivals or institutions for taking a stand.

Images of violence, of suffering, of death. Especially in *Guernica Guernica*—a performance that explicitly thematizes the visual culture of war and destruction—the question arises: What can we still show without merely repeating what already appears all day on news websites? A bleeding body on stage is no longer just a metaphor. It will be compared. With Gaza. With Bucha. With livestreams of death and mutilation that enter the theatre via social media even before the curtain rises.

In *Guernica Guernica*, FC Bergman explicitly addresses the question of representation. We are on a daily basis overflooded by images of violence, suffering, and death. The danger of becoming indifferent and numb is real. A crucial question for the theatre-maker is how to deal with these concrete images on stage if they want to address these issues. In the end there are only two possibilities: either the artist goes for realism or they look for abstraction.

FC Bergman confronts both options in *Guernica Guernica*. In the first part of the performance the theatre-makers go very far in the realistic representation of the bombing of Guernica and the material destruction and human suffering caused by it. This hyperrealistic representation—we see the explosions of the dropped bombs, we see the scattered and mutilated bodies—is a challenge for the public. How will it react? Will the audience perceive it as real and feel horrified by all that violence? Or will it merely see the theatrical tricks and techniques that are used to make it look real? Will it see the violence or its artificial construction? How will it respond emotionally and intellectually?

In his painting, Picasso made a clear choice. He went for poetic abstraction. But his representation of the cruelty in Guernica became so famous that the name Guernica refers, for many people, in the first place to the work of art and only in the second place to the destroyed city. You can even find a reproduction of the painting on a coffee cup! By confronting hyperrealism and poetic abstraction, *Guernica Guernica* opens a field of ethical questions on the artistic representation of violence, the emotional and critical responses to it, and the dangers of aestheticization.

Ambiguity

Within Toneelhuis itself, there is no singular line. They don't always agree with each other, certainly not on complex issues such as war and conflict. The stage as a place of dissensus. Not one voice, but many. Not one vision, but clashing perspectives. It's not always harmonious, but it is honest. And in that honesty, space emerges. For doubt. For friction. For tension that becomes fruitful.

There is always conversation. Always debate. That conversation is not optional—it is structurally embedded in how Toneelhuis operates today. In a time when many institutions remain hierarchically organized, their collective model offers an alternative that is both inspiring and exhausting. It is dissensus that the theatre breathes. Not as a problem, but as a method.

Artistic visions often clash. Opinions differ on political stances, aesthetic form, or audience engagement. Actors know they will never please everyone. But that's precisely the point. Toneelhuis does not try to merge—they try to resonate. Here echoes Chantal Mouffe's call for agonism: a model in which conflict is not resolved but acknowledged and played out. Where antagonism is not destructive, but at the heart of a democratic practice.

[redacted]

A theatre where doubt is still allowed, where ambiguity is not a weakness but a quality, where dissensus is not flattened into consensus but takes shape as an agonistic exercise. Perhaps theatre, in its fragile fiction, is one of the last places where conflict need not be resolved immediately, but may resound in its full complexity. Not a manifesto, but a space. No weapons, but words. And maybe that is the only weapon theatre has left: a place where contradictions are not avoided, but questioned. In an antagonistic world that craves clear positions, theatre offers something else: the uneasy, complex ambiguity of being human.

The rigid *What did you just say?*—the threat, the interrogation, the accusation, the coercion, the demand for a similarly rigid reply—is, in these performances, evaded, disrupted, dismantled, seduced, deflected... through artistic strategies: the proliferation of voices, the blending of disciplines, the dialogue between word and image.

Bipolar? Multipolar?
All in an effort to escape one-dimensionality.
Why not?

Artists have no spine to shatter.
They must, after all, live longer than violence.

Reference

- Oostrik, Johannes. 'Opmerkzaam en Nadenkend: Over de werkzaamheid van gebaren als dragers van een houding'. PhD diss. University of Antwerp, 2023.

[redacted]

Stay Upright

An Essay and Conversation with Theatre Company STAN on European Aesthetics, Cynicism, and Morality in Times of War

Pascal Gielen

The Belgian theatre company STAN has existed for more than thirty years. Since its founding in 1989, the group has developed a repertoire that consistently dissects power relations, violence, and moral discomfort: *JDX – a public enemy*, a raw reworking of Ibsen on hypocrisy and public truth; *Everything is Quiet*, on the aftershocks of war in the television living room; *Neoptolemos*, in which the remnants of Troy are transformed into moral debris; and *Klytaimnēstra*, where a mother's revenge claims its place in a world that offers her no language.

It is no coincidence that *Mitya* emerged from the same spirit—a performance created by Frank Vercruyssen together with pianist Emmy Wils. Central to the piece is Dmitri Dmitriyevich Shostakovich, the Russian composer who had to survive in silence under Stalin. The music is by Shostakovich himself—performed live. Vercruyssen: 'Let power reside in the music, for words cannot contaminate it. Music escapes language: that is its *raison d'être*, and its grandeur.'

Can music that deliberately touches the wound still soothe? Can theatre heal without comforting? Can ambiguity still be played in times of war? Can one be critical without becoming didactic? What does it mean when aesthetics refuses to moralize, but also refuses to remain silent?

With such questions in mind, I spoke with theatremakers Jolente De Keersmaeker, Damiaan De Schrijver, and Frank Vercruyssen at their rehearsal space in Antwerp. The occasion for our conversation was, among other things, their new production *Nachtland*—literally, 'Night Country'—a play by Marius von Mayenburg. It is a biting black comedy in which moral confusion takes centre stage. In an attic, hidden behind a pair of skis, a brother and sister find a painting signed 'A. Hitler'. What follows is not a process of purification or unmasking, but of moral entanglement. For what does it mean to inherit something tainted by history? What do you do with an image that would rather not be seen?

Initially dismissed as kitsch, the painting suddenly becomes charged with historical weight and economic value. The narrative spirals into self-denial, projection, blame-shifting, and cynical profiteering. And precisely in the tension between aesthetics and legacy, between image and guilt, the play touches on questions that extend far beyond the stage. Can theatre still mean something in a time when media images of war, violence, and loss inundate us daily? How do stylistic devices such as irony, ambiguity, and sarcasm function in a world where clarity is demanded—and where the line between irony and cynicism grows dangerously thin?

Inferno

The evening before our conversation, we watched the news: a five-year-old girl from Gaza emerged from the flames like a survivor from an ancient fresco—soot on her skin, yet seemingly unscathed. Physically, at least. But in her gaze, the abyss of the unspeakable. Her parents, brothers, and sisters had not survived. She alone remained, a silent witness to a world that had obliterated her future before she could even dream it. Do you still wonder where the embers of radicalization and violent fundamentalism are kindled?

Damiaan, with bitter sarcasm: 'We see that girl in the fire again every day. And next time it has to be worse: a body with its head blown off, or it doesn't work anymore.' That cuts—not because of the horror, which we've become used to—but because of the mechanism it reveals. What no longer functions is not the body, but the imagination. The visual culture itself has grown numb. Empathy seems subject to inflation. What shocked yesterday is today just another scrollable moment. Only images that stretch the unbearable even further—aesthetically, physically, morally—seem to penetrate public consciousness.

We live in a time in which violence must outdo itself to be noticed. A time in which children only seem to matter when they die in high resolution—sharp, saturated colours that do not obscure the blood, but amplify it. A time in which grief only resonates when it is 'streamable', repeatable, shareable—digestible within an algorithmic worldview. Ones and zeroes. Good or evil. Nothing in between.

The image as shock appears exhausted. The hyperproduction of visual violence functions as an intensified version of

[redacted]

trauma itself. Where once there was dismay and empathy, now remains indifference, avoidance, or denial. As Susan Sontag wrote: images lose their impact through repeated exposure. What once awakened conscience now deadens it. Images of violence no longer illuminate—they flatten. We become desensitized. Damiaan, dryly: 'We're numb.' Frank adds: 'We've reached the limits of what we can still feel through images. Shock? That's a matter of dosage. And dosage doesn't work anymore.'

In contrast, STAN presents the experience of theatre. Jolente stresses how fundamentally different it is: 'Theatre is the space where the body counts again. Where someone sits beside you. Where silence cannot be edited, but must be endured.' Theatre demands presence. While social media becomes ever faster, flatter, and sharper—every opinion shouted in caps, every image pixelated—theatre resists. It enforces slowness. 'That slowness makes space for reflection,' Frank notes. 'And that is essential today.' Damiaan sums it up: 'Theatre is not a confirmation machine, it's a thinking machine. You must stay seated, even when it chafes.'

But that resistance is not immune. Frank speaks of a 'permanent fog' we live in, 'the fog of capitalism. It's sprayed at us with enormous force by the media. And we go along. Inevitably. Us, too. A purgatory of images in which clarity becomes ever more seductive, because it offers direction amid the noise. Everyone shifts towards simplicity. The audience. The artists. Us, too.'

The market demands clarity. 'Choose. Position. Package. Sell.' Theatre that hesitates—that doesn't know, that refuses a label—is harder to market. A sitting duck. And they feel that, too: 'We're almost ashamed when we don't offer a clear message. When we have no identity, no mission, no label to attach.'

'We keep fumbling, doubting, stammering even. Because that's more human than slogans.' That stammering, that brokenness of meaning, is cherished. Murmuring. Against the backdrop of slick social media visuals, the stage becomes a space where failure remains visible—and invites thought. In discomfort, STAN recognizes a powerful ethical gesture. Jolente calls it old-fashioned, but vital nonetheless: believing in slowness, contradiction, incompleteness. Instead of turning the girl on fire into a viral icon, theatre allows her—through a different language—to remain a living human being in an uncertain inferno.

Moral Finger

In times of war, silence quickly becomes suspect. Those who do not explicitly take a stand seem to distance themselves. Especially artists, whose work enters the public sphere, are asked—or rather expected—to speak out. On Ukraine, on Gaza, on Congo. On who is right. On guilt. On victimhood. Artists appear to be asked more than ever to serve morality.

STAN rejects that kind of fanfare. Not out of indifference, but because they know how quickly an artistic message turns into a lie when it tries too hard to be understood. 'We're expected to draw lines, take positions, be clear and decisive,' says Frank. 'But what attracts me in *Nachtland* is precisely its refusal to offer us an escape.' No moral, no reckoning. Only clashing voices. And that is enough—or perhaps at least an honest starting point.

That doesn't mean there is no ethics in their work. Damiaan calls it 'preferring to search rather than to state'. Theatre as a circling gesture, not an assault. As a space in which doubt is not hesitation but a possible rhythm of life. Thoughtfulness resists being reduced to single-track thinking. It's not about transmitting knowledge or vision, but about a shared not-knowing. 'We don't stand above the audience. We show what we ourselves don't understand. And they recognize that.'

This is not an anti-authoritarian pose, but an attempt to return theatre to a communal ritual, where confusion is not suspicious but fertile. It confronts us with existential doubt. We are forced to look at ourselves before pointing the moral finger at someone else.

Unmasking

In the shadow of war, the stage easily becomes a tribunal. The audience waits for revelations. The villain must be identified, the hypocrisy exposed. Public shaming, now digital.

[redacted]

Theatre can deliver that too. Especially in morally charged times, the urge is great to tear off the mask, to reveal the other as liar or enemy of the people. Public Enemy. But what if that 'truth' is also just a facade? A farce, a face on Facebook. What if the fallen mask only reveals another mask?

Instead of digging for the one truth beneath the surface, STAN prefers to show how people hide behind layers they themselves no longer recognize. Characters do not speak in clearly defined motives, but in hesitation, slips of the tongue, diversions. They contradict themselves. Jolente: 'A person cannot be reduced to their beliefs—not even their actions.'

Unmasking becomes dangerous when it is presented as a purely moral project. From Brecht to Marx, from Freud to Bourdieu. From far-right to far-woke. The moment theatre, as Damiaan says, 'places itself above the other as a kind of moral awakening,' it ceases to be self-inquiry and becomes self-congratulation.

Performing Courage

No shock, no message, no unmasking then. What others wield as morality, revelation, or blow, STAN transforms into ambiguity. The language is plural, the gesture ambivalent. As life itself. This style is not new—it runs like a common thread through a body of work that continuously questions itself. A theatre born from a distinctly bourgeois culture—a culture at once inhabited and interrogated.

STAN's entire oeuvre might be read as a grand investigation into that bourgeois culture. A detective novel—not only in search of perpetrators, their behaviours and weaknesses, but also of the foundations on which citizens rest in comfort and complacency: the foundations of our speaking, singing, and thinking. In short: culture. Old European culture. What makes our reflection possible? On what grounds do our doubts grow? Our critical capacities? Even our claim to artistic freedom and non-binding autonomy?

Damiaan bluntly calls himself a 'leftist bobo'—a cultural petit bourgeois-bohemian who works and performs in a world that mostly puts itself on display. 'We rarely play characters we don't know. They're always citizens like us, confronted with their past in all its petty forms.' Frank adds: 'The reason we can make this work is because we have the surplus. We have the luxury to dwell in a cultural upper layer.' The luxury of critique and self-critique. Of irony and, yes, of cynicism too.

But that wealth has its roots elsewhere. In a past rarely looked straight in the eye. Congo is suddenly mentioned—not as anecdote, but as system. The colonial legacy embeds itself in our laptops and smartphones, in the machines through which we formulate our critiques, write our pamphlets, defend our artistic autonomy. The violence of the past continues to circulate as raw material in the present. The welfare state—and by extension, Western culture, science, and institutions—is built upon exploitation that never truly ended, only quietly modernized.

Congo thus becomes not history, but mechanics: first disrupt, then deny education, and finally accuse of moral failure. A cynical cycle repeating today in the United States, in Hungary, in Turkey—and perhaps soon all over Europe too. A spiral feeding inertia. Not innocent forgetfulness, but collective repression—maintained by a thin layer of political correctness meant to obscure deeper complicity.

Irony may at first appear as antidote—a way to undermine the greed and self-satisfaction of the cultural middle class. But it is fickle. What begins as playful self-criticism can devolve into complacent theatre. 'Look how critical we are.' The form becomes the alibi. Irony becomes a style that justifies itself, a smokescreen to avoid responsibility. What we call disarmament may actually be camouflage. Cynicism as the final stage of a class that no longer questions its privileges—but aestheticizes them.

Congo—like other postcolonial fault lines—functions as the repressed foundation of a civilization that neutralizes its conscience. We feed on it, intoxicated with self-justification. And that intoxication often bears a name: irony. Especially for the bobo-left, it's a comfortable refuge. No pacifism without this psych-political repression, gently wrapped in cultural finesse. That is precisely where it becomes precarious. Look at Germany today: seriousness returns. Irony loses its reflective power and

[redacted]

becomes a buffer against guilt. No longer a mirror, but a haze—a way to postpone confronting one's own complicity.

STAN is not innocent, either. The company plays with that bourgeois toolkit: irony, ambiguity, even sarcasm as strategies not to simplify the world—but also not to fully confront it. 'Irony is beautiful,' says Frank, 'but it can easily turn into sarcasm, and sarcasm is close to cynicism.' The difference is vital. Cynicism closes: nothing matters anymore. Irony opens: nothing is unambiguous. What appears on stage is not a moral truth, but a clash of perspectives. No verdict, but an invitation to reflect.

It is a fragile balance—and a deeply personal one. Frank: 'I think I've gone from red to dark red to black. The feeling that humanity needs to disappear from this world as soon as possible.' Yet he also expresses admiration for those who keep resisting: 'I admire that energy... until the very last breath. Noam Chomsky is like that. Howard Zinn, the Jewish-American historian who wrote *A People's History of the United States*, was still protesting a week before he died—for nurses' wages. Chomsky still believes in change. But I'm sometimes overwhelmed by the fatalistic thought: I don't want to invest my remaining time in that anymore. Sometimes I just want to lie on the couch and watch football. And fuck the world, because my time is running out.' That is a form of self-preservation—but it breathes the dark air of giving up. Of cynicism.

Damiaan pushes back: 'In my neighbourhood, Jews buy fish at a Moroccan shop. That still exists. That is hope.' In those small everyday gestures lives something stronger than cynicism: a belief in co-existence—despite everything.

To avoid crossing that line, something is needed that one might call 'performing courage': to stand on stage against all odds. 'You have to keep playing,' says Damiaan, 'even if you know you're preaching to the choir, even if it feels lazy sometimes.' Jolente: 'For me, personally, the very fact of stepping onto a stage and trying to stay in dialogue—with each other, with your audience—is proof that you're not cynical. It means you still want to stay upright.' In that sense, continuing to perform is not just artistic persistence—it is moral resistance.

Irony, then, is not escape, but a way to inhabit complexity without flattening it. Not a refuge, but a strategy for survival—on stage, and beyond. Performing courage is what remains at the edge of the abyss, where meaning trembles and where politics and image cry out for clarity. Stay upright. It is not a grand gesture, but a modest act of persistence: continuing to speak into silence, continuing to look where others prefer to turn away. To stand on stage as an act of stubbornness. To climb the stage again and again—against the hysterical media stream. A vain attempt to keep standing on the world orb, even as it ominously rolls towards the abyss.

References

- Bourdieu, Pierre. *La Distinction: Critique sociale du jugement.* Paris: Les Éditions de Minuit, 1979.
- Brecht, Bertolt. *Brecht on Theatre: The Development of an Aesthetic.* Ed. and trans. John Willett. New York: Hill and Wang, 1964.
- Chomsky, Noam. *On Power and Ideology: The Managua Lectures.* Cambridge, MA: South End Press, 1987.
- Freud, Sigmund. *Beyond the Pleasure Principle.* Trans. Caroline Jane Mary Hubback. London: The Hogarth Press, 1920.
- Ibsen, Henrik. *En folkefiende (Een vijand van het volk).* Copenhagen: Gyldendal, 1882.
- Marx, Karl. *Das Kapital: Kritik der politischen Ökonomie.* Hamburg: Otto Meissner Verlag, 1867.
- Mayenburg, Marius von. *Nachtland.* Frankfurt: Verlag der Autoren, 2008.
- Shostakovich, Dmitri. Symphony No. 5 in D minor, Op. 47. Musical composition. 1937.
- Sontag, Susan. *Regarding the Pain of Others.* New York: Farrar, Straus and Giroux, 2003.
- Zinn, Howard. *A People's History of the United States.* New York: Harper & Row, 1980.

[redacted]

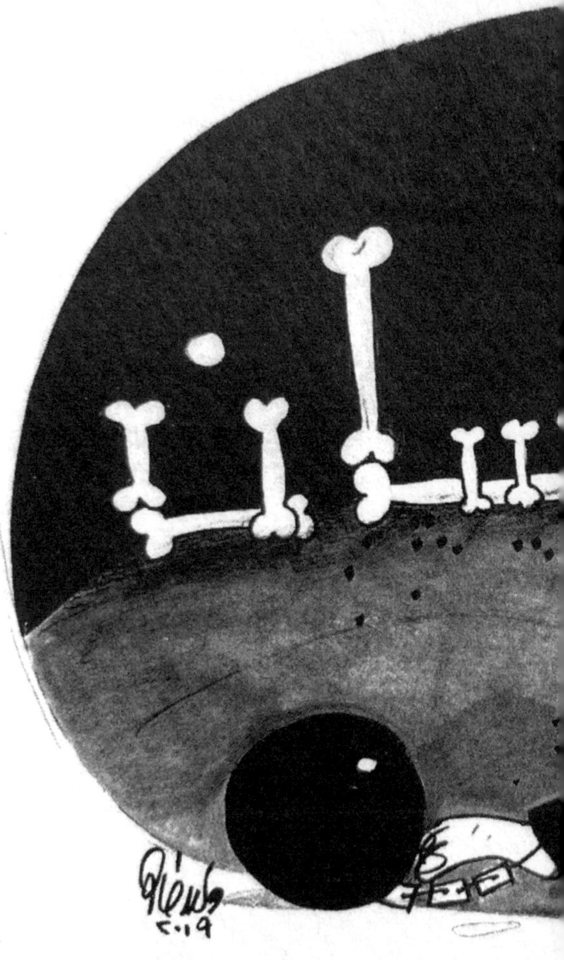

Walid Taher, *Human Rights*, 2009, drawing in which the word 'human' is held up by a man while the word 'rights' is spelled out using human bones

حقوق

Torn Between Bombs and the Absence of Bombs

[redacted]

The Vertical Gaze

Interview with Diana Al-Halabi

Emily Van Driessen
Jan Beddegenoodts

Diana and I met in early 2025, when I interviewed her for the 'Prospects' exhibition by the Mondriaan Fund at Art Rotterdam. Born in Lebanon in 1990 and based in the Netherlands since 2020, Diana works across film, painting, and installation. Her multidisciplinary practice navigates the entanglement of the personal and the political, challenging top-down structures of power. She goes from the patriarchal gaze and institutional violence to bureaucracy, settler colonialism, migration, and the everyday realities of displacement. Whether addressing hunger as a weapon of subordination, the sanitized vertical violence of drones, or the silent grief of migrants, her work resists aesthetic neutrality. She moves between media instinctively, guided by urgency: film when language must act, painting when words fall short.

In just one hour, Diana left an immense impression on me. We had a conversation that moved me to tears of both sorrow and joy.

Sorrow, because the weight of what she addresses is heavy, and she speaks about it with such extraordinary clarity and generosity. Joy, because throughout our conversation, a tiny parakeet named Bubu fluttered around her, chirping 'Kookikoo, I love you', pressing kisses onto Diana's mouth. A persistent life force amid heavy realities.

After that meeting, Diana's reflections echoed in the corners of my mind, and later resurfaced in conversations with filmmaker Jan Beddegenoodts. It felt almost serendipitous when we realized that Diana's ongoing artistic research intertwined so naturally with the questions that *In the Absence of Bombs* is exploring.

Across different countries, cities, and mediums, it was as if we had been participating in subconscious collective research. We are deeply grateful to have been welcomed once again into Diana's atelier in Rotterdam, to continue a conversation that surpassed anything Jan and I could have imagined finding words for.

—Emily Van Driessen

When we spoke the other day, you mentioned how your relationship to language, film, and painting has evolved over time, and how language fails in moments of collective trauma or genocide. How has this shaped your practice?

Diana Al-Halabi • My practice is shaped by resisting top-down structures. That means oppressor versus oppressed, colonizer versus colonized, verticality versus horizontality. And I usually start from the deeply personal, and then trace the lines outward, towards the larger political frameworks in which the personal is entangled. But in my film *The Battle of Empty Stomachs*, the process was reversed. I was trying to juxtapose two types of political hunger. On one hand, famine: a top-down mechanism of state violence, imposed on the people. On the other hand, hunger strikes: resistance from below, initiated by individual prisoners as a form of protest. For this project, I moved into ethnographic research for the first time. I interviewed Palestinian hunger strikers who had survived something I could never truly understand. I arrived with carefully prepared questions, rooted in theory, but the very act of questioning made me realize how far removed theory is from reality. No matter how generously they answered, the visceral gap between experience and understanding remained.

So I thought: How dare I try to speak of something I could barely comprehend? I treat any film that deals with collective trauma with utmost care, and I don't want to sound like an artist who thinks I am entitled to speak of other people's pain just because I have a platform or so-called pedestal. And yet, they didn't see it that way. In Cairo, someone told me: 'Thank you for making this film.' And that made me realize: sometimes it's not about entitlement. It's about who is holding the megaphone.

While I was making this film, the forced starvation of Gazans by Israel escalated. Making a film about hunger while witnessing a genocide in real time was overwhelming. That's when I began to question language itself and

[redacted]

how complicit it is. The tongue, after all, is the organ of speech and also the first organ of digestion. In the film, I staged that confrontation directly. My mother tongue speaks in Arabic, asking me: 'What do you know of hunger?' And my answer was: 'I know nothing. I only know fasting.' And that feels indulgent compared to what others endure. So I reached a point after the film where I needed to step away from language, at least for now. I needed to find a place where I wasn't translating trauma into something comprehensible, especially for people who will never come close to living it.

During this time I also became deeply interested in aphasia, the loss of language after a brain stroke. I heard a woman speak about it in a podcast; when she started getting her words back, she missed the time she was without language. Because even the richest vocabulary could never fully capture the sensations of shock, grief, mourning, trauma. That's why all these synonyms of pain or genocide don't equate. Nothing ever will. That realization echoed Lacanian psychoanalysis: the Real is precisely that which cannot be captured by the law of language. So how could I pretend otherwise? Language is confined, constrained.

That's why, for now, I'm taking refuge in painting. With painting, I don't feel the need to explain. In film, especially with voice-over, there's always a kind of navigating, and I enjoy holding the hand of the viewer and walking them through a maze of thoughts and feelings. But with painting, I'm not navigating. Painting became a space for ethical discomfort. If what I paint feels comfortable, I feel uncomfortable. It has to be uncomfortable. So I reside in painting for now. Maybe that's a way to come close to 'the Real', in Lacanian terms.

How do you choose an artistic medium when you know what you're trying to express might be impossible to contain?

DAH • The medium I choose is always dictated by the

urgency of the subject matter. If I'm speaking about something that is happening right now, I have to respond differently than when I'm dealing with something from the past. That's why I move between different mediums.

With *The Battle of Empty Stomachs*, I chose film because I wanted to thoroughly explore the issue, drawing from both historical records and the present. I use language extensively in my films, but I didn't want to rely solely on spoken words to speak about something I didn't fully understand. So I used visuals, sound, choreography, and transformed the answers of the interviews into a poetic dialogue.

It became a carefully woven complexity where each element carried a part of what could not fully be said. One scene, for example, shows a high dining table towering above. It symbolizes the state. Beneath it, on one side, someone tries to reach the food, but can't, representing those subjected to state-imposed famine. On the other side, a political prisoner can reach the food but chooses not to eat, embodying the hunger strike, where the digestive system becomes a political battleground and a last resort for claiming one's rights.

I'm sure I failed to contain everything. Because it's impossible to contain a disaster in a film, an artwork, or any medium. Which, in fact, is also the title of my previous film: *The Disaster Cannot Be Contained*. No matter how much we try.

In 2021 the urgency of the moment meant stepping into performance. My peers and I created a banner that read 'Stop the Ethnic Cleansing of Palestine', because we wanted to protest the forced eviction of Palestinians from Sheikh Jarrah by Israeli settlers. When we tried to hang it from the university building, we were told nothing could be attached, and they removed it. But we kept hanging it, and they kept removing it. So instead, I thought, let's call it a performance—Holding Palestine—and hold it by hand. We held Palestine for seven days, and people across the Netherlands signed up to hold the banner, hour by hour in ten-hour shifts. It

[redacted]

became a form of living resistance.
At the time, it felt very urgent. But I also started to realize that not every form of resistance moves at the same pace. Sometimes you need to look back, or around, and make a film. Sometimes you need an even slower pace, a solitary act, so you paint.
I believe we are now living in times of action. But resistance isn't one single act. It's cumulative, stretching across many frontiers, both in the West and in the places where the bombs are falling. You have to choose your medium of resistance. Maybe right now it's standing in the street. Maybe it's fighting a university dean. Or maybe it's documenting what's happening.
Still, I fear sometimes that activism or protest can become a gesture, something symbolic. Even the Aboriginal Tent Embassy, the longest [continuous] protest in the world, which I deeply admire, makes me wonder: When does a movement become a monument?
I think about whether it's time to find new tactics. Maybe economic resistance. Maybe something else entirely. And even though it's never enough, trying matters. And I salute everybody who's trying.

During the 'Prospects' exhibition at Art Rotterdam, you told me a story that revealed how abstraction can lead to different interpretations. Could you share that again?

DAH • In Rotterdam, I tried an exercise with one of my paintings, *Clean Cut*. I wanted to see if I could speak about it without mentioning Palestine, and if people would still grasp the layers underneath. The work speaks about how violence gets sanitized in so-called 'civilized nations'. If a bomb drops from the sky and kills 500 people, it's seen as a clean, distant death. But when someone kills with a knife, it's up close, direct, and is seen as barbaric. It's about the difference between vertical and horizontal violence. In 1935, Bertolt Brecht wrote an essay called 'The Five Difficulties of Writing the Truth', where he compares people who are against fascism but not against capitalism to people who like to eat their veal without seeing the calf being slaughtered. But as long as the butcher washes his hands, they're fine with it. It's a form of guilt-washing.

So I'm standing near the painting, explaining these ideas without naming Palestine, and two people were listening, one from Argentina, one from the Netherlands. Then one of them said, 'Ah, that makes a lot of sense. I'm vegan. When I see these bodies, I think that if people actually witnessed how calves are slaughtered, they would stop eating meat altogether.' The other one agreed: 'Yes, if killing animals was televised, shot live, people would definitely stop eating meat.'

And I just stood there, watching this interpretation unfold, completely missing the genocide happening—only a scroll away. I eventually said, 'Yes, you're right. And now, we're witnessing a televised genocide happening in Palestine.' They nodded, awkwardly, and said, 'Yes, you are right, that is also true. Anyway, we have to go now.' And they left. It made me realize again that solidarity is a choice. It's not a question of visibility or abstraction. The images are there. The testimonies are there. You can choose to see, or you can choose to look away.

I also started questioning my own role in this dynamic over the past year. I used to translate everything into English when I shared stories. But then I asked myself: Why? Do I really believe the white world will save us? Is it really necessary to keep translating pain into their language? No. It's not. So I stopped, and I started sharing in Arabic. If someone wants to understand, they will take the initiative to translate. It's not my role to be an educator.

You said that seeing is a choice. In today's world, we're constantly bombarded with images of suffering, war, and loss, and many vanish as quickly as they appear. You called this 'scroll amnesia' in our previous interview: the way we keep watching but forget almost instantly. What happens to violence when it becomes an image?

[redacted]

DAH • We live in a time where war isn't remembered. It's refreshed. You scroll. You click. You move on. And it's not because we lack access to information or images. It's about who is considered worthy of living, and who is not. When I am scrolling, as we all do, I feel the need to click, to keep looking. Out of guilt, because I'm safe. One time I came across a video. It showed a group of murdered Palestinians lying on the ground. And on top of them, there were cats. Three bodies, maybe, and six cats, just sitting there. I stared at the screen and wondered: Are they grieving? Sleeping? Eating? Keeping the bodies warm?

I took screenshots, instinctively. I knew the footage would disappear. Maybe in hours, maybe days. Even if I searched for it later, no keywords would bring it back. In the past, images of war used to carry memories. You could see a photo and know: Vietnam, Iraq. Now, even the memory itself is slipping away. Quick, quick, quick. So a painting is a way to document things that can slip away into the abyss of the internet.

And I started asking myself: Do I have the right to paint this in order to document it? To be honest, I don't know. I don't know if we have the right to restage it through art directly, because if seeing the real image didn't move you, would an artwork? We don't need a softened, aestheticized version of pain in order to act.

Once, I was in a talk and a director told me, 'I can't wait for the films that will be created from Gaza.' And I asked, 'Why? We already have all the images'. And she said, 'Because with music, people will be able to digest what's happening.' And I said, 'No, they don't need to be able to digest it. You don't need to soften the edges for the so-called "civilized" in order for them to be able to look at the violence that they have initiated.'

So in my practice I ask myself: Should I show images as they are, or should I abstract them? Especially since I don't know the names of those in the images, and the ethical questions around exhibiting pain are many. I've chosen to abstract. I'm still figuring out what the right way is to be in solidarity. But at least I'm trying. Because silence is not the solution.

You are now developing the project The Vertical Gaze: العين المجردة *in connection to* Fragments of the Real. *Both projects started in 2025 and are still in their early stages. Can you tell us about each project, and how a vertical gaze became a recurring concept?*

DAH • In *Fragments of the Real: What Happens When Migrants Sleep?*, I recently began researching and documenting the invisible dreams of migrants living removed from their homelands under attack. The project began with my own dream moving from the personal towards the political.

When the bombing in my homeland, Lebanon, intensified, I dreamt I was visiting a Lebanese friend, but the dream took place in Gaza. Missiles started falling around the house. While her family remained calm, my fear was out of control. I felt very shy that I was panicking so loudly. When I woke up, I couldn't help but wonder: Am I dreaming this to bridge the gap of displacement? Was I trying to be there?

So I shared that dream online, and then the messages started flooding in. People I didn't know, scattered across Europe, wrote to me: 'I dreamt the same.' Different versions. Same fear. Same places. I also dreamt I was shouting 'Free Palestine' at Ben Gurion Airport, even though I've never been there. A friend told me she also dreamt she was at that airport, wearing a keffiyeh around her neck. She twisted it to hide the pattern, terrified they would arrest her. That's when I realized: these weren't just individual dreams. Perhaps they formed a shared collective unconscious. An invisible reality which, if collected, could form a counter-archive of diaspora with *Fragments of the Real.*

Right now, I'm painting those dreams. It's my way of making a statement without using my immediate voice. I've also started recording people as they narrate their dreams. Maybe the project will evolve into something else. But for now, documenting feels like the most honest response I can offer to what art should do. We're living through a time that demands armed resistance, and as an artist I recognize my limitations. My capacity can only go as far as the medium allows. So this is my resistance.

One of the gestures that kept appearing in the dreams was the act of looking up. That marked the beginning of *The Vertical Gaze*. In Gaza, in Beirut, or even within the collective memory of migrants, you look up because danger often comes from above. I remember walking in Beirut, and passing two delivery guys standing under a tree. There was a rumble and one of them asked the other: 'Is it a bomb?' I said, 'No, it's thunder', and kept walking. But that moment stayed with me. Here, in the Netherlands, you would never mistake thunder for a bomb, or a generator for a drone. Over there, you do.

Painting the vertical gaze holds all of that: the anticipation of violence, the memory of survival, the verticality of fear. In my previous work too, as in *The Battle of Empty Stomachs*, you can also see figures reaching upwards, unable to touch what's above them. Or in my graduation project, *On Scales of Violence: How to Measure a Dictator*, I used anthropometry, ergonomics, and the verticality of a child's gaze to speak about power structures within the family unit. I then juxtaposed this with the somatic and astral measurements of a dictator who reaches you from above, through satellites, bombs, and news. All to speak of who has access, and who is made accessible.

There's always a hierarchy in that vertical movement. Sometimes you're looking up for bombs, sometimes for help, sometimes you're begging for money. Sometimes we look up in fear. And sometimes we look unfazed, as if to say, 'Okay, you want to bomb us?' There are many layers in that gaze.

You started these projects from a place of distance, watching a war unfold from supposed safety. Even without bombs falling, you describe another kind of war. What kind of violence persists in the absence of bombs?

DAH • There are different layers of violence. There is physical war, and there is psychological war. I'm geographically safe in Rotterdam, and that is a privilege, one I fought hard to acquire and keep. But every decision has a price. And we pay it viscerally as migrants. Sometimes it's in the neck, the stomach, the heartbeat. Sometimes it's in our dreams. It's as if you're in fight-or-flight mode, but there is nothing around you to fight or flee from. I'm not comparing it to reality in the homeland, but rather to the so-called normal life of the host country. There's this constant shame for feeling afraid here when others are dying over there. Shame for carrying trauma, even when you're not under physical attack. We're not allowed to fall apart. So you silence yourself. But at the same time, there's this constant sound of the news, where correspondents barely breathe between one word and the next. Even their pauses are filled with murmuring. There is no silence. Not even for a fraction of a second.

In the host country, no one asks how you sleep or how you carry those dreams in your days. They are asking if you fit the bureaucratic requirements for a visa or for citizenship. What is asked of you dismisses the double reality you're living in. Bureaucrats can't see the bombs you were just under in your dreams. They can't see the news that's scrolling through your fingers while they're drafting their policies; that's where bureaucracy becomes a form of violence.

Can you imagine being expected to learn a new language immediately in the integration process, while your brain forgets whether you bought yoghurt today? Can you imagine staying up until 4 a.m. because the Israeli military posted a warning on their X account to evacuate a building just next to your sister's house?

And the ceasefire would start at 4 a.m. So you wait all night on the phone with her. You say: 'Please wake the kids up.' And she says: 'What if they don't bomb it? I don't want them to live this fear.' Then it's 4 a.m. You whisper, 'Mabrouk, congratulations, they didn't bomb it.' And the ceasefire begins, on paper. But did the risk really vanish? Can you imagine having to wake up the next day and go to meetings and appointments in a very safe environment?

Even though it's a privilege, it feels like being trapped in a safe space. It's what Frantz Fanon called the split of the subject. You're living a schizophrenic reality: a double life where your body is 'safe', but your mind is elsewhere, with violence at an arm's length away in your phone. That's why I call it being a 'psychological refugee'; you seek refuge, but mentally it's not possible. You're displaced geographically and emotionally.

So I've been trying to document this invisible war to create a counter-archive of this displaced life that is supposedly uprooted, even though our roots are still aching and acting. There are bombs shelling in our dreams, while we walk in silent streets. But again, this pain is not even a fraction of the horror our loved ones endure back home. This project is geographically and conceptually placed in displacement.

When I first arrived in the Netherlands, I realized I had tinnitus. I had never heard that much silence before. It was when I learned: violence could be silent too. I knew how to live under clear, immediate violence. But the bureaucratic and social coldness, that was a new kind of violence altogether. This is the invisible war. And it speaks to the unconscious of the migrant, which I think is worth documenting.

How do you cope with the split reality of living in diaspora?

DAH • Through art, definitely. And sometimes through humour, because it's the only thing that truly matches the

irony of what we're living. For example, in psychoanalysis, there's this Lacanian idea of 'talking to brick walls' that really started to resonate with me. During analysis, an analysand speaks to an analyst who doesn't give any input. It can give the feeling as if you're speaking to a brick wall. The silence is said to help you surpass a certain threshold, allowing you to tap into the Real. And now I often joke: as migrants, we live this every day, without ever stepping into a therapist's office. You speak, but the system doesn't really listen. You explain, and there's no response. I even turned this concept into a painting.
Or, when I applied for Dutch citizenship and I told my friend, 'I'm applying for neutralization.' She laughed and said, 'You mean naturalization.' But I said, 'No, I meant it. I'm already natural. They're trying to neutralize me!' That's what this whole process feels like. It instantly reminded me of Gloria Wekker's idea of white innocence. So if one day you see me and I no longer have a stance, then you'll know. They succeeded—I've been neutralized [laughs].

Left Right
Drawings and Selection of Poems

Mohamed Hijji

[redacted]

The following illustrations and poems are from the book *Shimal, Yemin* (*Left, Right*) by Egyptian artist Mohamed Hijji (1940–2023). In military marching, 'left, right' is a cadence call, indicating which foot should be striking the ground during a step. The book was published in 1982 while the artist was living in Tunisia. Following several abrupt political changes in the Arab world and the rise of Western funded military dictatorships, Hijji felt the need to critique this reality with illustrations and complementing poetry. The book has a selection of black and white illustrations by Hijji, paired with poems by prominent contemporary Arab poets. The poems in this selection are by Palestinian and Iraqi poets whom Hijji chose because they were critical of the war machine and its operators. Even though some of these poems were written over fifty years ago, they still hold true today. Mohamed Hijji was a prominent designer, artist and illustrator. He collaborated with many publishers in different parts of the Arab world. His book *Shimal, Yemin* is banned but he made it freely available to the public during the 2011 Egyptian uprising on his social media page after changing its name to *al-'ar* (*Shame*).

Hide

And under the stars of those who led you, hide
In the books. Coffeeshops. The bar. The brothel.
            Political games.
The fall of poets. The elite league. Petrol. Women's hips.
The gay's apartment. Hotel halls. Political party appointment.
Spy school. Execution room.
And in everything you have ever loved. Hide.
So that you don't see the face of the raped girl
And her body torn to pieces.
And divide, while he dripped, we filled twenty graveyards.
And thousands of barracks.
Raised on our twenty flags.
Engraved with every bullet that killed one of our sons.
And every stone in every house that has been turned into a
            prison.
I say:
For her. Hide.

—Saadi Youssef

[redacted]

Mohamed Hijji, illustration with poem by Saadi Youssef, from *Shimal, Yemin*, ink on paper

فاختبئوا

وتحت نجوم من قادوكم إختبئوا

وفي الكتب . المقاهي . المشرب . المبغى . ألاعيب السياس

سقطة الشعراء . نادي النخبه . البترول . أرداف النساء .

وشقة اللوطي . قاعات الفنادق . موعد الحزبي

مدرسة التجسس . غرفة الإعدام ..

وفي كل الذي أحببتم إختبئوا

لئلا تبصروا وجه التي أغتصبت

وقطع جسمها قطعا

وفرّق — وهو يقطر — مالئا عشرين مقبرة

وآلافا من الثكنات

مرفوعا على راياتنا العشرين

منقوشا بكل رصاصة قتلت فتى منا

وكل حجارة في كل دار حولت سجنا

أقول :

لأجلها إختبئوا

« سعدي يوسف »

The police are looking for my head in the desert
And here I am without a history or refuge
I move from one step to the other
And I feel like I am the murderer and the murdered
Because I am the murdered without my knowledge
Forever slaughtered, Oh! Country
Slaughtered in wakefulness and dreams
Slaughtered except in newspapers and the rulers' radios
Who has a drop of water?
Who knows a river for rent?
Who knows poets
Who do not wait at the door of the sultan?
Who knows a country where humans are not slaughtered?

—Mustafa Muftaqir

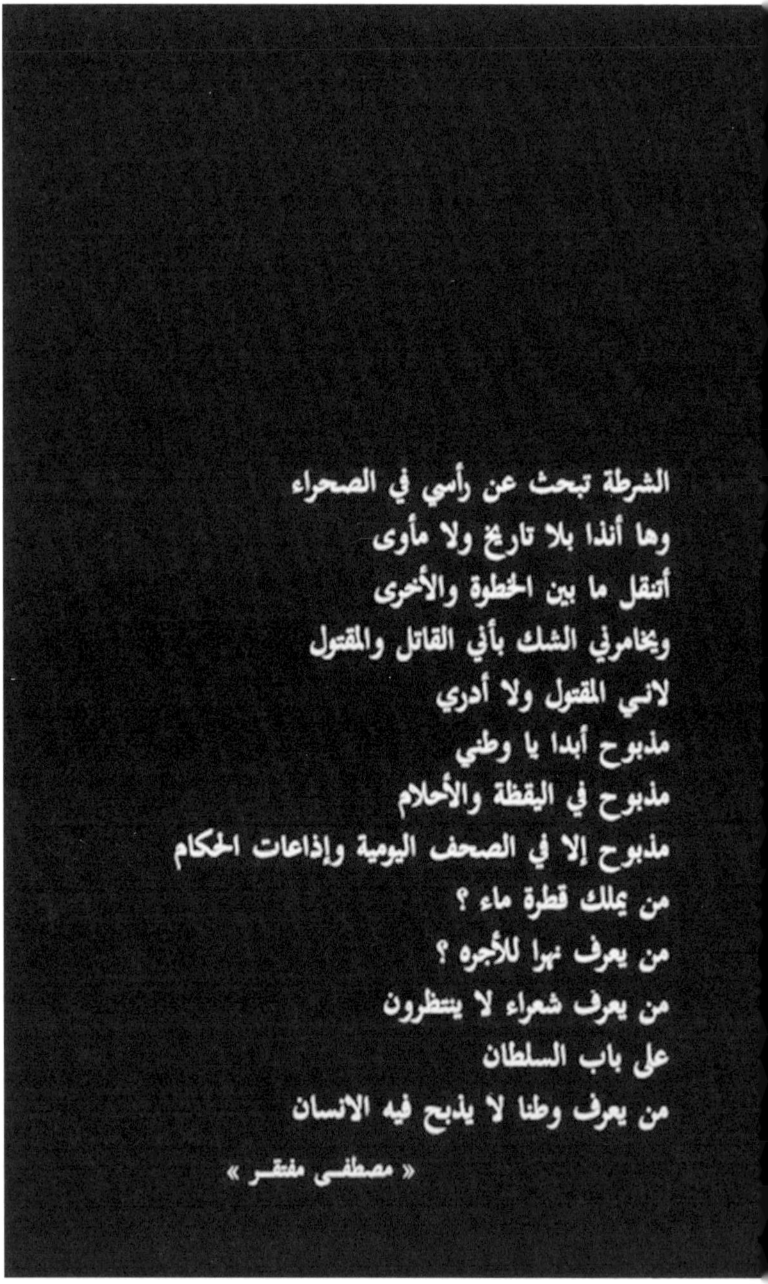

Mohamed Hijji, illustration with poem by Mustafa Muftaqir, from *Shimal, Yemin*, ink on paper

Even my wounds and my heart beats surprised the soldiers
They surprised everything that was not dead even in a
    graveyard
They surprised me like you surprise a fruitful palm tree
A flock of hungry birds in a brazen village
The eyes of rifles eating my path
Legitimacy fire dreaming of my crucifixion
****
After they nailed me and I cast my eye towards the city
I almost didn't recognize the field, the fence and the graveyard
It was something, as far as the eye could see,
Like a flowering forest
In every eye sight was a cross and a crying mother

—Badr Shakir al-Sayyab

[redacted]

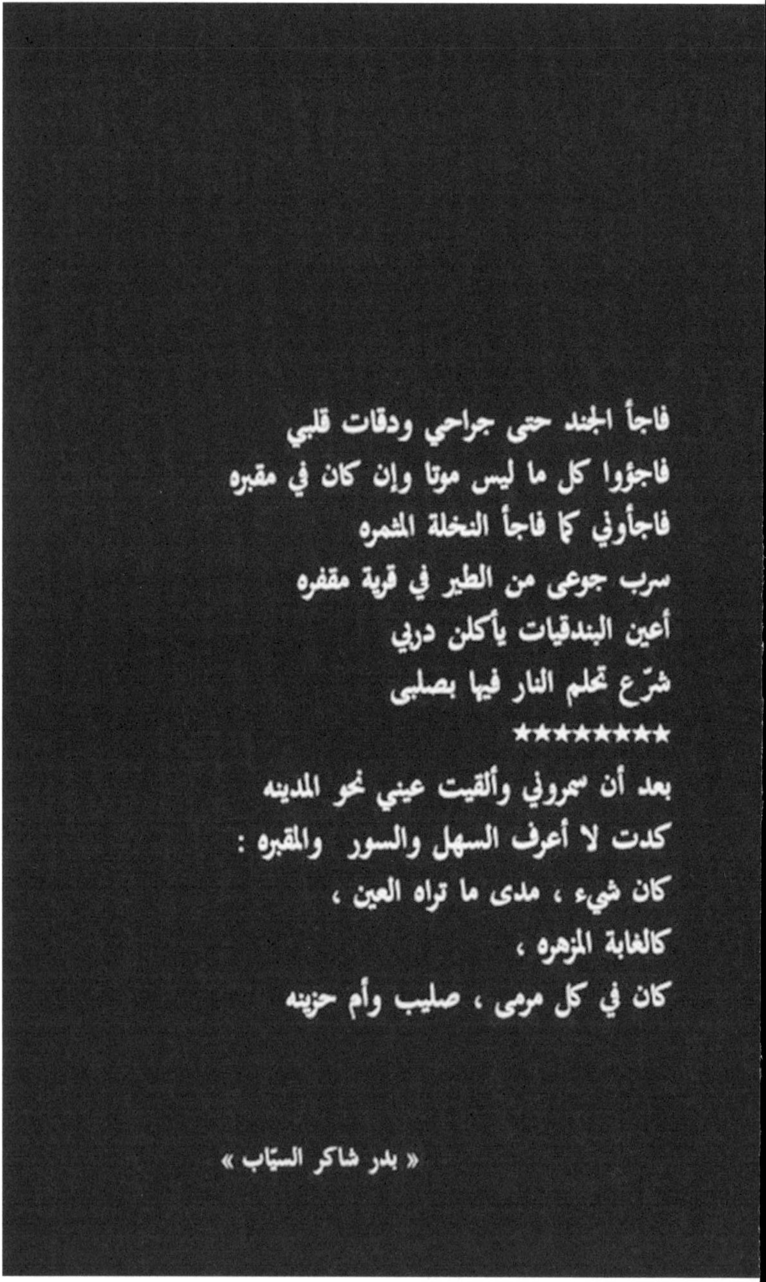

Mohamed Hijji, illustration with poem by Badr Shakir al-Sayyab, from *Shimal, Yemin*, ink on paper

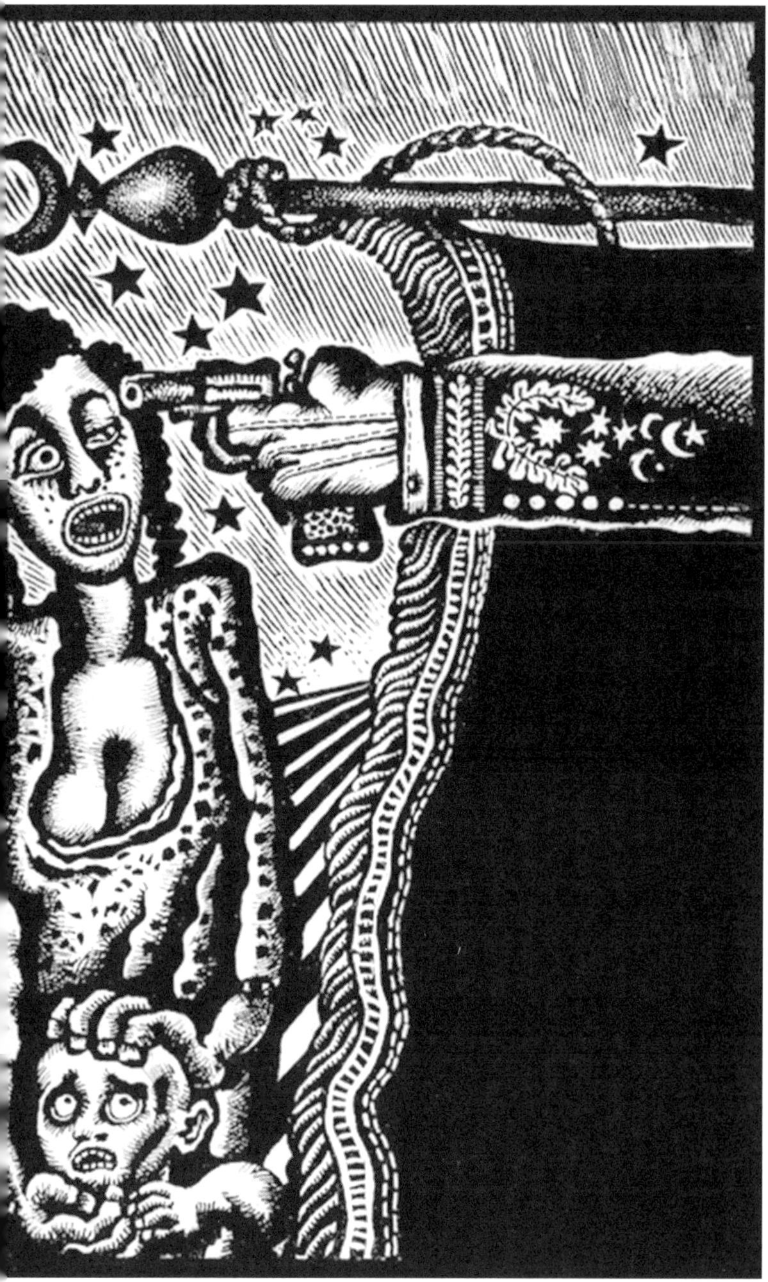

This is the era of perjurers
****

The big nations
Generals
Machines
Oh Father why haven't you raised your forgiving hand
In the face evil that is approaching from all doors
Why do you deny words?
Love turns into torture?
And silence torture?
In this exile and the words become
A lifebuoy?

—Abdul Wahhab Al-Bayati

[redacted]

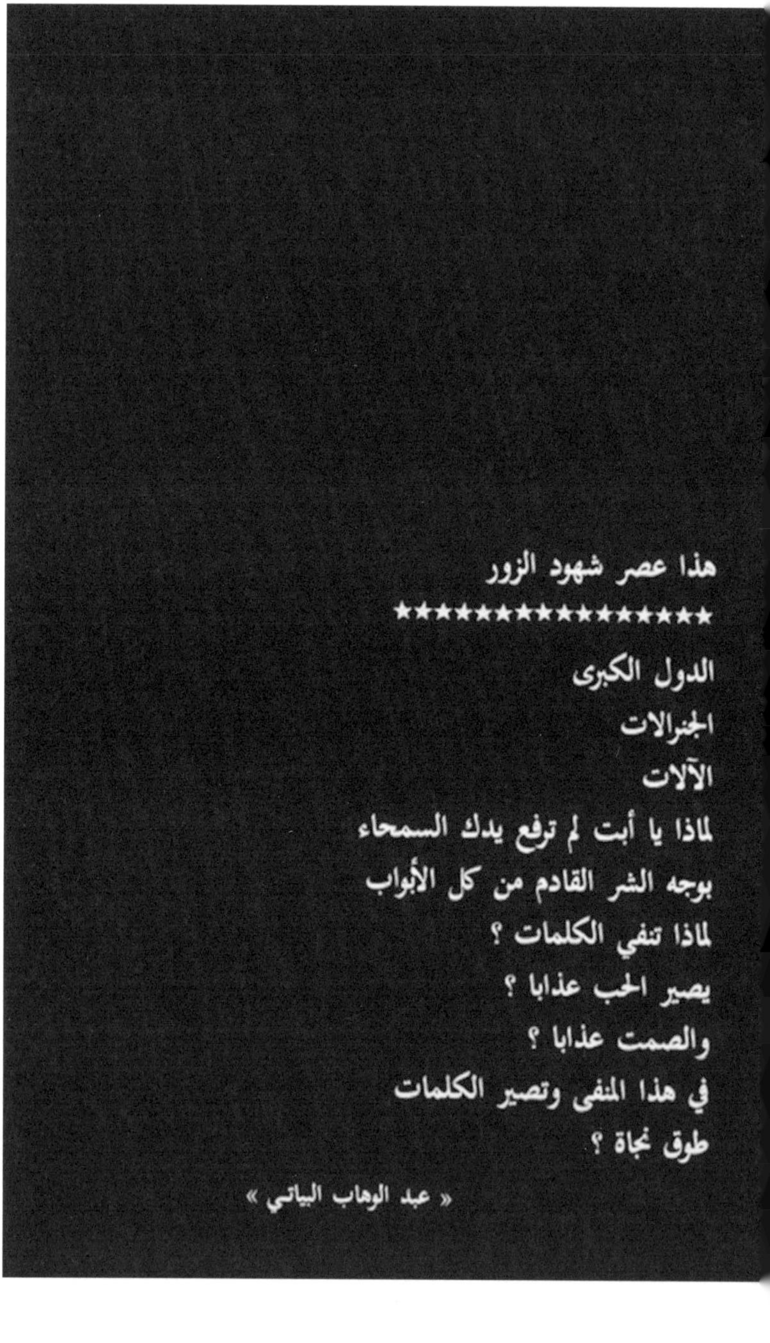

Mohamed Hijji, illustration with poem by Abdul Wahhab Al-Bayati, from *Shimal, Yemin*, ink on paper

A grey horizon scattered in the horizon
Roads made out of round shells
Not roads
And from the ocean to hell
From hell to the gulf
And from the right
To the right
To the middle
I only saw gallows
I saw gallows with one rope
For two million necks

—Mahmoud Darwish

[redacted]

Mohamed Hijji, illustration with poem by Mahmoud Darwish, from *Shimal, Yemin*, ink on paper

أفق رصاصي تناثر في الأفق
طرق من الصدف المدور
لا طــرق
ومن المحيط إلى الجحيم
من الجحيم إلى الخليج
ومن اليمــين
إلى اليمــين
إلى الوســط
شاهدت مشنقة فقط
شاهدت مشنقة بحبل واحد
مــن أجــل
مليوني عنق

« محمود درويش »

How filthy we are! How filthy we are!
How filthy we are! And big headed! How filthy we are!
I don't exclude anyone
Do you confess to the morality of the street and barracks?
And to licking the thigh stuck to the nightclub's door?
Oh audience of the night, who are regulars in the institution of
frivol
We will be the Jews of history
We will howl in the desert with no shelter
Is it a country ruled by royal thighs?
Is this a country or a brothel?
Is this land earth
Or a den of wolves?

—Muzaffar al-Nawwab

[redacted]

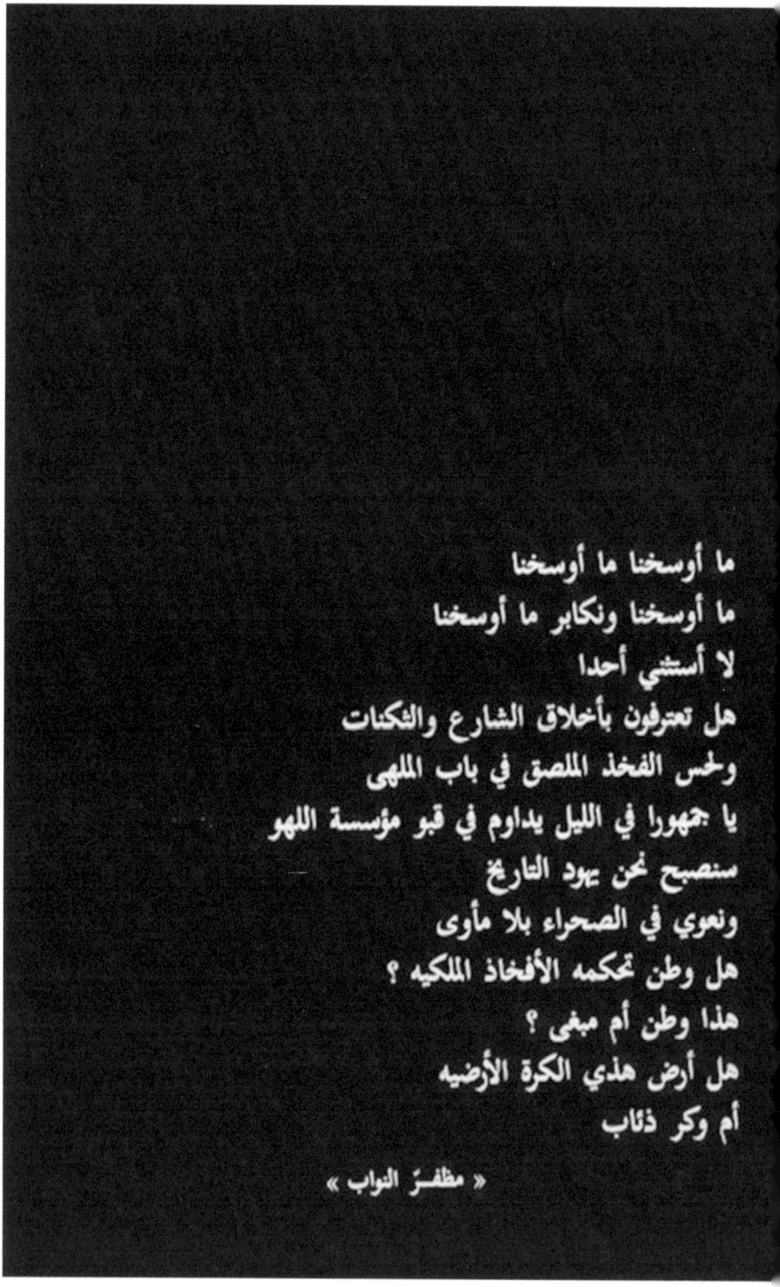

Mohamed Hijji, illustration with poem by Muzaffar al-Nawwab, from *Shimal, Yemin*. ink on paper

One day they surprised me
They pushed my mother and
sister aside
And they detained me
On mud and barbed wire
They dragged me all night
But my head was kept high
I was a field of wounds
And a red flag
A pamphlet of struggle
When the door creaked in
some of the prisons
Before the break of dawn
Without the blink of an eye
They killed me

—Samih al-Qasim

Mohamed Hijji, illustration with poem by Samih al-Qasim, from *Shimal, Yemin*, ink on paper

ذات يوم فاجأوني
دفعوا أمي وأختي جانبا
واعتقلوني
وعلى الأوحال والأسلاك
جرّوني طوال الليل
لكن ظل مرفوعا جبيني
كنت بستان جراح
راية حمراء ..
منشور كفاح
حين صرَّ الباب في بعض السجون
قبل ميلاد الصباح
وبلا رعشة هدب
قتلوني

« سميح القاسم »

Sohail Salem, *Untitled*, Deir al-Balah, 12 October 2024, ink on paper

Our Lives Have Become Lines

Sohail Salem
Annelys de Vet

We sat at the harbour of Gaza, on a terrace at the pier, drinking tea and looking out over the beach—crowded, overflowing with people. Families sat on blankets in the shade of colourful umbrellas; vendors moved back and forth selling snacks and ice cream; children played in the waves; and further out at sea, boats—often brightly painted—bobbed on the water, with fishermen standing tall, braving the swells. We shared salty peanuts that the artists I was sitting with had just bought. The afternoon sun cast a warm glow on their faces, and each detail around us seemed to spark imagination and a cheerful anecdote.

Laughter brought a sense of relief, a moment to breathe after I had spent the entire day holding my breath while driving through the Gaza Strip in the aftermath of the 2014 war. I witnessed not only the brutal destruction of buildings and infrastructure, but, more profoundly, the devastation caused by the ongoing siege. It wasn't just the physical ruins that weighed on people's minds—it was the blockade preventing building materials from entering, making reconstruction impossible, piling onto the destruction of previous wars and the decades-long illegal military occupation. Many were forced to live in the remnants of collapsed homes, with no alternatives. Reality choked, leaving no space for breath.

I was sitting at the pier with artists Mohamed Abusal, Sohail Salem, and other founding members of the Eltiqa Gallery in Gaza City. Abusal and I had organized a workshop together, and throughout the week the participating artists visited various carpenters, potters, weavers, tailors, furniture makers, and social workshops where people gathered to craft products together. Their practices were stunning, passed on through generations, their histories ingrained in their produce. I vividly remember—amidst the devastation around us— their joy, love, and imagination, as well as their generous hospitality. Art could not save Gaza, but it saved these individuals, their children, and their families. It gave them a way to express their stories, practice hope, and imagine other, brighter futures—despite the overwhelming darkness.

In the summer of 2022, the Eltiqa Gallery was presented at Documenta 15 in Kassel with a selection of their artworks and an annotated timeline of their activities. Some of the artists had been able to travel to Germany, and their stories, reflections, and realities were amplified for global audiences.

Their exhibition was curated by the Palestinian collective The Question of Funding and aimed to rethink the economy of funding and how it affects cultural production both in Palestine and the world. The Eltiqa collective was a sheer example of how to work together, build community, and, through art practices, develop sustainable economic models in one of the most unstable environments.

More than a year later, the gallery was destroyed entirely—bombed by the Israeli occupation forces. Nothing left. The artists had been violently displaced, and later, they heard that local people had entered the ruins, salvaging paintings and furniture to make fires for warmth and to bake bread. The artists mourned the loss of their artworks, yet they asked: 'What is the meaning of art now? Aren't people's lives far more important?'

This did not stop them from creating; art was their lifeline. During the ongoing genocide, Sohail Salem shared his work on social media, with drawings that captured what no line could outline.

—Annelys de Vet

Sohail Salem, *Endless Lines*, 21 December 2024, ink on paper

Sohail Salem, *The Mother*, 21 December 2024, ink on paper

Endless Lines, 21 December 2024

Endless lines stretch, our faces showing fatigue and despair. We stand patiently, our eyes weary. We stand motionless, our blood freezing in our veins, and time killing us as it passes excruciatingly slowly. Our words are too heavy to describe this line. We all unite in this scene, and social differences fade. The sounds of shelling in the background, ambulances, and the tired whispers of the elderly drift into our ears with the sound of the wind through the line. Our lives have become lines.

The Mother, 21 December 2024

The mother sat, taking shelter in a dilapidated tent, hugging her family tightly, fearing she might lose one of them. Her tent, like any other, neither protected them from the cold nor shielded them from the shrapnel of the bombing. Her eyes told the story. Safety: where is it? Amidst the chaos of war, the destruction of homes, and the loss of loved ones. The mother is a symbol of resilience. She tries to hold herself together and appear strong in front of her children, but her heart freezes from the cold and the horror of the bombing. Yes, she is the mother, a star lighting the way.

These are drawings with ink pens on school notebooks, expressing the hope for an everlasting light despite the constant noise of aeroplanes flying over Gaza and the sounds of explosions, which cause headaches, lack of concentration, and sometimes even temporary memory loss.

I did not migrate to the South at the beginning of the war, despite the extreme danger, but the occupation army arrested me when they stormed my residence in Gaza City, in the southern neighbourhood of Al-Rimal. They separated me from my family, forcing them to flee on foot to the city of Deir al-Balah. This was on 18 January 2024, 105 days after the war started.

The soldiers interrogated me while I was handcuffed and blindfolded, and they wrote a message in Hebrew on my forehead. The men around me whispered about the meaning of the letter and whether it meant the army would kill me first.

After long hours of interrogation, they released me to walk for about seven hours. I also arrived in the city of Deir al-Balah. After two days of searching, without any evidence or information, a call led me to my family's location.

My main priorities included buying groceries and paying the rent for the garage where I lived, which is very challenging due to exploitation and high prices. And there's no place to work; everywhere, it is chaotic, and with my family, it is crowded. I bought simple drawing tools from a street vendor in Deir al-Balah. The small notebooks and pens have been my refuge, and I placed them in my small bag without worry, as if I were writing my memoirs daily.

Every day, a story or a tale inspired me with one or more drawings. My first drawing was of a violet flower, and then I asked the good fairy to turn it into a rose. With courage, her fellow violets did not dare to do so, based on the story of the ambitious violet by Gibran Khalil Gibran. It is the violet that did not pay attention to betrayal and intimidation.

I began drawing in Deir al-Balah. It was my mission to release a visual story of the misery I had stored in my mind, which was most brutal when I was forced to pass over the bodies of martyrs during the displacement. The idea of drawing seemed

[redacted]

ridiculous. What could I draw in such circumstances? And why? My brain was damaged from the sounds of intense bombing that kept on resonating in my head. But every morning, I tried to separate myself from my surroundings, overcrowded with displaced people, by listening to the news on the radio at high volume and sketching with ink pens. My small, sharp, and disturbed drawings encapsulate fear and anger in a narrow notebook space.

The quick sketches had a sense of calm; you need to consider in which context these artworks were produced. They are more than just the distribution of colour on white paper; they are a state of internal accumulation that I express as a miniature portrait of my condition, ambitions, hopes, and pain.

With trembling hands, I have tried to draw them without hesitation and post my sketches on social media whenever I have the opportunity. I never planned for this to be met with so much approval from my friends, and for them to share my stories further. The cold blue artworks ignited and grew hotter from the interaction with my friends.

Many of my friends, relatives, and neighbours have disappeared. The beautiful Gaza has been destroyed. My drawings are a message to the world, a scream for help, and a message to my remaining friends that I am still well. In February 2025, I went to the hospital twice and was diagnosed with pneumonia. I am getting better now and will try to draw again soon, but my psychological state is very bad from the war. I am waiting for it to stop.

—Sohail Salem, Gaza City, March 2025

Sohail Salem, *Untitled*, Deir al-Balah, 4 December 2024, ink on paper

Sohail Salem, *Breaths Under the Rubble*, Deir al-Balah, 12 October 2024, ink on paper

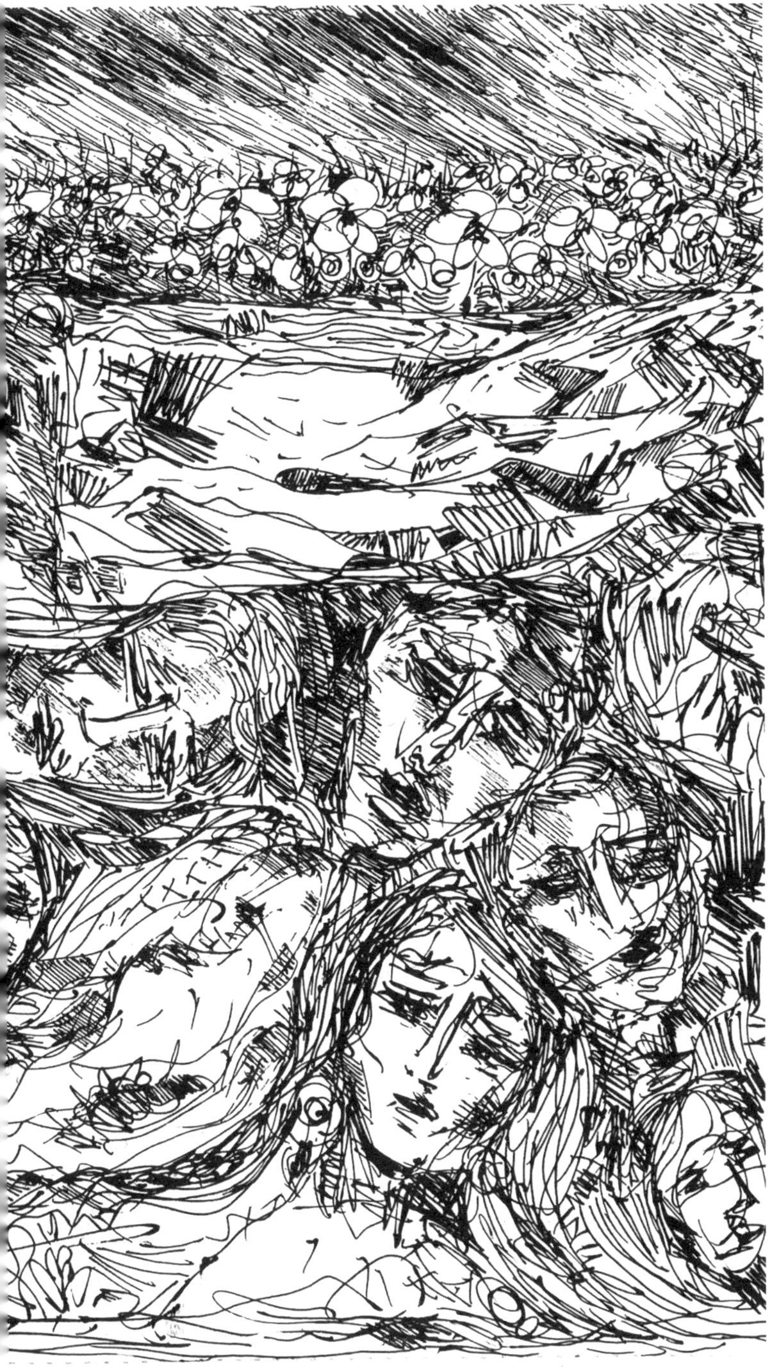

And Tomorrow, We Will See Death Again

Amir Ashkar
Jan Beddegenoodts

[redacted]

Dear Amir,

Been a while since we talked, you have been in my thoughts...
It's impossible for me to find words for the horror that we are witnessing in Gaza right now. Could I publish some of your Insta posts in a new book that we are working on?

Jan dear, hope you are well. Sorry I have been away a little bit. Been in my cave, looking to find words for what is happening. Not an easy task really.

Please do. Share my thoughts.

Lately, I've been writing more and more — for a book I am hoping to publish soon — but honestly it feels like shouting into a vacuum. Except of a few friends, around here I feel surrounded with deaf ears. Muted timelines.

Sometimes I get stunned when I speak and find people actually listening, understanding my words — not necessarily about genocide but just normal conversation. I am stunned that they understand. How is that possible? How can we share the same species, breathe the same air, while some of us are being slaughtered and others go on with ordinary lives?

This dissonance... it's beyond me. But please share. Communication is extremely important, and it's the least we can do now...

Thank you Amir

Could you send me your Bio please🙏

Amir Ashkar is a Palestinian philosopher, winemaker, and activist whose work explores time, trauma, and identity. He is currently pursuing a PhD on the relationship between Being and festivals in Nietzsche's thought. Amir is from the displaced community of Iqrit and the co-founder of Return, an initiative that reclaims original homes without waiting for the occupiers' approval.

Jan Beddegenoodts, *Chat with Amir Ashkar,* screenshot from a conversation on Signal, 2025

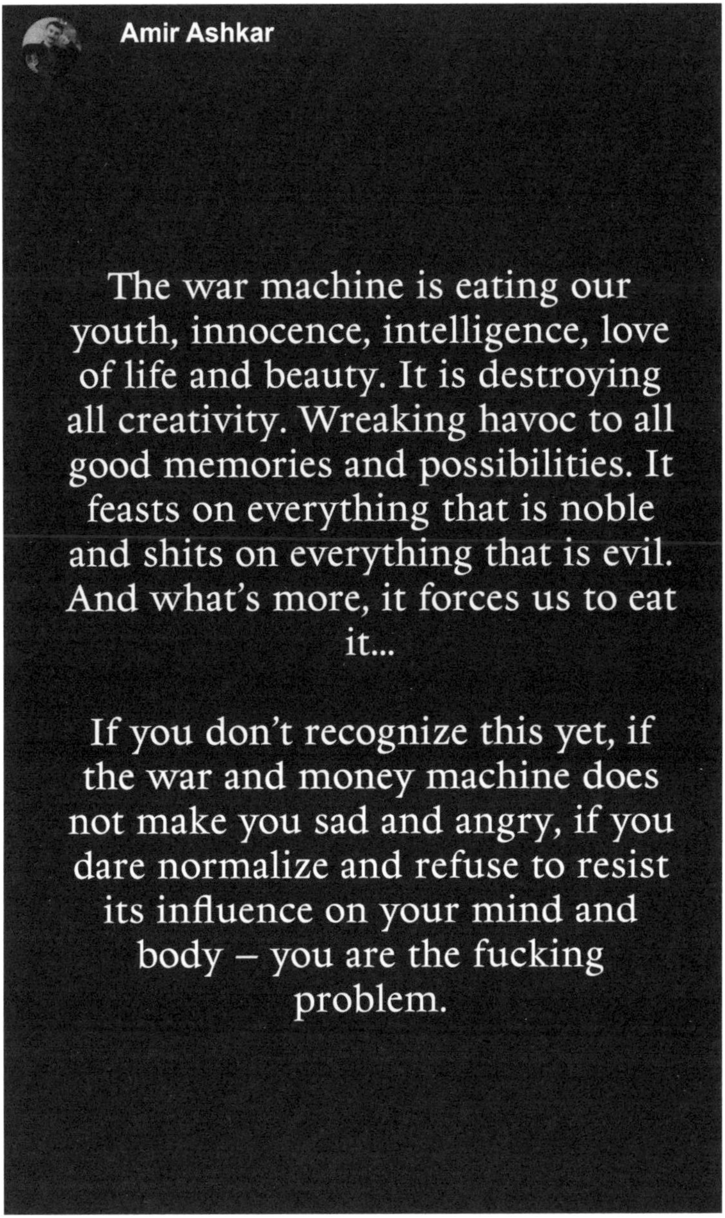

pp. 193–197: Screenshots of Amir Ashkar's stories on Instagram, 5 April 2025

Amir Ashkar

What does it feel like to be a student in a place where the shadow of genocide darkens the colours that you see, the sounds you hear, and the very air you breathe? To sit behind a keyboard in an attempt to trace letters in order to produce words that now seem a world apart from you?

How can one make sense of the absurd symbols of knowledge while the weight of history crushes you from all sides: and the anxiety of an uncertain future leaves you hanging on the verge of an abyss...?

Can you truly learn when you see soldiers in uniform, students with machine guns, all around you?

Amir Ashkar

But it is not merely the weight of the gun or the presence of soldiers that renders our thought difficult, but the suffocating sense that our mind is also occupied, that it is unable to explain to the death-machine that carries the gun what the hell it is doing.

For what does truth at all count if we cannot use it against those that ruin life and the value of life?

Indeed, how can one's thoughts ascend, how can the spirit flourish, when everyday is an assault on the very right to think, to act, to exist even? The mind, trapped within such violence, becomes a prisoner of its own need to survive, of its own pragmatism, and cowardice. Like the land beneath your feet, like the sky above your head, your body here is also occupied.

Amir Ashkar

To be a student in such a place, is to carry within you an infinite heaviness, a long period of suffering that is neither past nor future but a troubled present that seems to have no end in sight.

I tell you, it is not easy to grapple with abstractions - equations, formulas, philosophies - it is not easy to read Nietzsche or Freud when your existence is reduced to something completely disposable.

When the horizon itself shrinks before a gigantic wall of oppression, it becomes extremely difficult to concentrate. You need to be a fucking lunatic in order to do that. Maybe I am a fucking lunatic ...

Amir Ashkar

We see death all day. Children torn to shreds. Men flung into the sky by bombs. Women with their bellies cut open, their entrails exposed – to those who care and to those who don’t. This is not a war. It is the theatre of erasure. It is a genocide performed in real time, for a world that scrolls past.

The stink is everywhere.It fills the lungs. It seeps into the soul. And the ones who do this? They walk freely. They taste wine and laugh. The Israelis go on as if their hands are not soaked in blood – As if no one could see.

But I see.

We see.

And we – what do we do? We post. We perform grief in high resolution. We beg the algorithm to make pain trend. To maybe spread the "message". As if witnessing alone could halt the machinery of annihilation. As if saying "genocide" often enough could undo the pain of it.

But it won't.

It doesn't.

And tomorrow, we will see death again.

We will post again.

Drawing Between the Sirens

Making Art During Wartime, One Day at a Time

Interview with Gamlet Zinkivskyi

Jan Beddegenoodts

When I first met Gamlet Zinkivskyi in the winter of 2023, it was in Kharkiv, a city under constant bombardment. I was filming *Gamlet*, a documentary tracing his survival as an artist in wartime Ukraine. Now, in February 2025, I meet him in a different setting: the Swedish Army Museum in Stockholm, where his work is part of an exhibition. The contrast could not be starker. No missiles, no air raid sirens—just an unsettling silence.

Much has shifted since that winter I filmed in Ukraine: in our personal lives, in Ukraine's scarred landscapes, and in the global order. Donald Trump is back in the spotlight. Europe hesitates, caught between pacifist ideals and the cynical realities of geopolitical power play.

How do artists navigate the uneasy space between resistance and political instrumentalization, between mourning and action? How do aesthetics shape narratives of suffering? And what role can culture play in rebuilding fractured societies? These questions hover over the conversation with Gamlet, whose work exists in this contested space.

Gamlet, a prominent street artist from Kharkiv, has used art as a form of resistance since 2014, when Russia first invaded Ukraine. Over the years, his work has evolved from occasional murals into a deeply personal and political practice. One of his most significant projects, 365, is an ongoing visual diary—one drawing per day, chronicling both the mundane and the horrific realities of war. And it's from within that space—between resistance and ruin—that our conversation unfolds.

—Jan Beddegenoodts

Your project 365 has now spanned over a decade. Can you explain what it means to you?

Gamlet Zinkivskyi • When the war began in 2014, I was faced with a choice: either take up arms or channel my resistance into art. I chose street art. If I was going to stay in Kharkiv, I needed to make my presence felt through painting. Before 2014, my work was sporadic. But after the invasion, it became a mission to reclaim the walls of my city.

[My project] 365 started in 2013 as a simple artistic challenge: one drawing a day for a year. But when the war broke out, it became something much more. In 2015, as the conflict intensified, I repeated the project to create a sense of stability and continuity in the middle of chaos. Since then, I have returned to it every two years—2017, 2019, 2021, 2023, and now in 2025. Each series documents the shifting landscape of my life and my country: shelling, loss, survival, hope.

Sometimes I imagine walking through an exhibition in 2034, seeing all ten editions of 365 displayed together—spanning twenty years of war and survival, drawn day by day. That thought alone keeps me going.

How does 365 help communicate the war's realities to those outside Ukraine?

GZ • News reports don't always connect. After years of war, many in Europe have become numb to images of destruction. But when people see my 365 drawings—some showing missile strikes, others capturing small, fleeting moments of beauty—they step into my world. They experience the war not through headlines or statistics, but through daily life.

Of course, I know no drawing can fully show what it feels like to live through war. The sudden impact of a missile. The unpredictability of survival. These are things you can only truly understand if you've lived them. Still, 365

[redacted]

is my attempt to bridge that gap. Even if it's imperfect.

Has the war changed how audiences react to your work?

GZ • Definitely. Before 2022, my street art was just that—art in public spaces. Some people liked it, some didn't. But after the full-scale invasion, the response changed completely. One piece from that time, *Keys Miss Their Doors*, went viral. It showed keys—symbols of home—floating in the air. Many Ukrainians who fled still carry the keys to homes that may no longer exist. When I painted that mural, I wasn't thinking about impact. But people began sending me photos of their keys, saying the work helped them feel connected to what they'd lost. That made me realize: street art doesn't need to reach millions to be meaningful. Even if it speaks to one person, that's already enough.

How do you view the media's portrayal of war? How does your work differ from mainstream narratives and images?

GZ • I've met an incredible number of journalists from around the world—from well-known publications to small outlets I had never heard of, and probably never will again. I respect everyone who comes to Ukraine despite the risks, whether to Kharkiv or even the front lines, to document what's happening here. Some of them do remarkable work, risking their lives to tell the truth.

At the same time, war coverage can feel like a media battle: Who can show the most horrifying image? Who can find something so terrifying it gives people goosebumps? I understand that this kind of reporting draws attention. But it often reduces war to shock value: numbers, strategies, distant explosions.

I try to tell a different story. My work isn't about explosions; it's about what's left behind. When I paint inside a bombed-out building or write something on a destroyed bridge, it's not just art. It's a marker of presence. A way of saying: someone was here. Life continues, even in ruins.

That's also how people outside Ukraine encounter my work. Even those who aren't as engaged with the war sometimes come across it—because of images that circulate, because of coverage that reaches far. I know that, in part, it's thanks to foreign media that my work has found a broader audience. But when they see my pieces, they don't just see destruction. They see that a street artist is painting in these conditions, on these surfaces. That matters.

I also work with objects that soldiers pass on to me—things you would never come across in civilian life: fragments of downed planes, a torpedo with an unusual propeller, bullet-riddled helmets, torn body armour. They ask me to turn these remnants into artworks—pieces that can help raise funds for urgently needed equipment: drones, repairs, protective gear. That has become part of my daily work.

The hard part is having to remind people again and again that these fundraisers still exist. The so-called 'civilized world' seems tired of the war. But we're still in it. And at times, it feels like the world is standing just one step away from collapse.

War, in reality, is personal. It's the moment you realize that the building you passed every day is now rubble. It's waking up to the news that a friend you spoke to yesterday is gone.

As an artist, I try to show what the media can't—the weight of loss. Where a report lists how many missiles were launched, my drawings show the spaces that they left behind. Where headlines discuss negotiations, I draw the absence of those who never got to see the outcome.

My work doesn't follow a format. It doesn't need to balance objectivity with engagement. It doesn't aim to be neutral. It's personal. Direct. Emotional. And that's why it resonates differently.

In a couple of days, you will be creating an artwork in Brussels about Europe's slow response to the war. Can you tell us about it?

GZ • For the cynical third anniversary of the full-scale invasion, I was invited to create a piece at the European Parliament building in Brussels. My first idea was simple but not feasible: to tape every window with the cross-pattern tape Ukrainians use before airstrikes. The message would've been clear: 'While you delay your response, this might become your reality too.'

Instead, I created a work called *How Many Times*, made up of sixteen short statements—each starting with that phrase. 'How many times I have heard sirens. How many times I have lost a friend.' The piece is meant to confront. Not to comfort politicians, but to make them feel the weight of delay and inaction.

It's a deeply personal project. Before the trip to Brussels, I struggled with the idea of being part of such an institutional setting. What could I possibly say to people so far detached from our daily reality of war? That's when I turned to the *Smile Mask*—a grotesque half-mask made by my friend, the artist Bob Basset.

It covers the lower half of my face in a permanent, eerie grin. I told him about the diplomatic events where I'd be expected to smile, to stay composed, even while carrying everything that weighs on us inside.

I'll wear it while I install the piece. It's my silent protest—an unspoken commentary on the performative diplomacy dominating the discussions of Ukraine's future. The *Smile Mask* has become a physical embodiment of that paradox: the pressure to appear calm and civilized while carrying the unbearable weight of war inside.

Here I am, creating art about war in a city untouched by it. Where life carries on, where meetings take place behind closed doors, far removed from the urgency we live with every day. Still, I remind myself: if even one person sees the work and truly understands what is at stake, it will have been worth it.

Do you believe art can still make an impact?

GZ • I do. I keep painting. I keep working on 365. I'll keep creating new murals, in Kharkiv and beyond. Even if my work doesn't change how Europeans see the war, it matters to those of us living through it. When people look back on this time, I want them to see more than ruins and battle reports. I want them to see that in the middle of destruction something was created.

I understand that art cannot stop the war. But it can document it. It can prove we were here, that we fought, that we lived through this. Every day, I wake up and draw. Some days, I don't know if I'll live to finish the next page. But I keep going.

In war, time feels different. A single day can feel like a lifetime—full of fear, survival, and sometimes even unexpected joy. That's what 365 is really about. It's not just about war—it's life inside war: exhaustion, resilience, even the absurdity of painting on streets that might be bombed the next day. It's about trying to stay sane. Trying to make sense of the chaos.

People sometimes ask me why I keep going. The truth is, I don't know how to stop. Stopping would mean giving in to everything we've lost. As long as I can paint, I will. That is my role in this war: to make sure that when all of this is over, something remains beyond just destruction.

Do you have hope for Ukraine's future?

GZ • Victory doesn't just mean the war ends—it means we win on our own terms. Not through deals made by global leaders who tell us to lay down our weapons. I want Ukraine to truly win. That's what matters most.

If we do, we won't just survive—we will transform in ways no one expects. Even now, in the middle of war, there's incredible momentum. Ukrainians don't postpone. They act. That's why we sometimes laugh at how slowly Europe moves. There's no war there, yet everything moves at an

[redacted]

unbearably slow pace. Here, even as cities are destroyed, people keep building, working, creating, fighting for what's ahead. That resilience will drive us forward after victory.

I don't care about my career as much as I care about victory. One day, I want to walk through Kharkiv and see it fully rebuilt, alive again. That's the dream. Until then, I keep drawing. Tomorrow, I'll add another page to 365.

Gamlet Zinkivskyi, *Loves Me, Loves Me Not*, 2023. © Gamlet Zinkivskyi

Bob Basset, *The Smile Mask*, 2025. © Bob Basset. The mask is worn by Gamlet Zinkivskyi

The Smile Mask*: Hamlet's Grin in Times of War*

For Serhii Petrov, known in the art world as Bob Basset, masks have never been mere objects. They are thresholds between selves—shifting identities that reveal as much as they conceal. Once created for the spectacle of music and fashion—worn by Slipknot, Metallica, and the avant-garde—his masks now carry the weight of war, bearing the scars of history in their very materiality.

The *Smile Mask* embodies the paradox of expression: a smile that isn't necessarily a smile, a grimace that could just as well be despair. It stands as a perfect emblem for a world where the performance of resilience masks the slow erosion of the self. In war, as in theatre, the face one presents becomes a survival mechanism—a shield against what lies beneath.

'Haven't heard you say thank you once,' said J. D. Vance to Zelensky. Perhaps Zelensky could have worn a *Smile Mask* in the Oval Office—or maybe, in a way, he already was.

Basset's practice has shifted. He now forges masks for soldiers who have lost an eye, transforming absence into presence, trauma into testimony. These are no longer masks for masquerade, but for necessity—prosthetic, protective, and profoundly symbolic. More than ever, his materials speak. Spent shell casings, remnants of destruction, find their way into his work, embedding the violence of the present into the artefacts of the future.

If, as Adorno feared, art risks aestheticizing horror, Basset walks the finest of lines—ensuring his masks do not simply represent war, but bear its weight, its fragments, its irreparable wounds. In a world where tomorrow remains uncertain, his hands continue to shape meaning. To hold on to the thread of creation is, for him, an act of defiance. Art, in this reckoning, is not escape but engagement—a refusal to let the unspeakable remain unspoken.

We're Still Alive, So Remove Us from Memory[1]

Asynchronicity and the Museum in Resistance

Lara Khaldi

The museum in resistance is not as we imagine: a material structure and archive of a past struggle of emancipation. It is rather the generative collective disintegration of this material in the struggle for forging collective myths. The museum in resistance is a museum outside of time, as time is always controlled by the hegemonic power. It is a museum which does not reserve a record nor a trace, but rather a shared knowledge in continuous circulation and transformation.

Take One: The Museum Object in Battle

In her essay 'A Tank on a Pedestal: Museums in an Age of Planetary Civil War', Hito Steyerl writes about a military tank that was stolen from the pedestal of a Second World War monument in Ukraine and used in battle during the 2014 conflict.[2] Borrowing from Giorgio Agamben's work on the relationship between civil war and stasis, Steyerl accuses the museum of being the site—perhaps even the engine—for a history which keeps returning and remains stuck in a loop. She defines the kind of history that returns by the re-use of the tank as 'partial, partisan, and privatized, a self-interested enterprise, a means to feel entitled, an objective obstacle to coexistence, and a temporal fog detaining people in the stranglehold of imaginary origins.'[3] In other words, the exhibition of the tank on a memorial site is complicit with this history, as it embodies it, makes it available and visible, causing its return. Following her argument, the museum functions as a time travel machine that hurls us back in loops of violence: 'The museum leaks the past into the present, and history becomes severely corrupted and limited.'[4]

A national museum works under the assumption that its objects are representative of its citizens, tacitly equal and homogeneous. However, this only continues to aggravate residual tensions. Civil wars thrive on historical tensions, and are usually propelled by national, ethnic, or religious binaries, which mask class struggle and injustice caused by the ruling national bourgeoisie.[5] Still, the museum presents itself as a public institution, and the objects within it as owned by the citizens of the state. Exhibitions in this sense become a means for the representation of the nation. Thus, it is not illogical for citizens to re-use its objects. Once the objects are exposed and re-used, the museum's time seeps out of its doors, infecting all its citizens, trapping them into a loop.

The birth of the modernist museum has always been associated with revolution, with the Louvre as the emblem of this history. If the museum is post-revolutionary, it is also post-colonial, as it is often one of the first institutions to be built post-independence. In the Palestinian context, however, time outside the museum is still under settler colonialism, and resistance to this is still underway. So, while the debate around decolonizing the museum is rooted in a 'postcolonial time', the colonialization of Palestine continues, and the struggle against it ensues as an elongated present. We therefore find ourselves in an uncanny situation where we suffer the symptoms of a new post-independence nation-state, with new national museums, local authorities, and a neo-liberal economy, while still under settler colonial rule and without sovereignty over land, people, or infrastructure. Considering this asynchronicity with the temporal rhythms of the national and modernist post-revolutionary museum, what happens to the objects within it, and how do they remain active in the present?

Take Two: Fugitive Objects

The Yasser Arafat Museum in Ramallah exhibits a number of weapons, some with a symbolic provenance. One such weapon is the personal pistol of the late Yasser Arafat. Another gun belonged to the late Khalil al-Wazir (Abu Jihad), co-founder of the Palestine Liberation Organization and commander of the armed wing of Fatah. Yet there is a stark difference in the ways the two pistols are exhibited. While the pistol of Arafat is displayed behind museum glass, near the famous speech he gave at the 1974 UN General Assembly, Abu Jihad's is only represented by a photograph. Arafat's pistol has had a symbolic function ever since he spoke the most famous lines from his 1974 speech: 'Today I have come bearing an olive branch and a freedom fighter's gun. Do not let the olive branch fall from my hand.'[6] Almost fifty years later, encased in museum glass in Ramallah, the pistol is evidence of the death of that revolutionary era for the leadership. It represents the trigger for the museum's present-day politics; collaboration with settler colonial powers through censorship, repression, and security coordination.

The picture of Abu Jihad's pistol, on the other hand, is like a hole in the museum. From this crack, present-day reality seeps in. Underneath the photo, the label reads: 'The gun was obtained from the family of the martyr but the museum has not yet been able to bring it from Gaza.' Abu Jihad was assassinated in 1988 in Tunis by the Mossad. The pistol carries traces of the assassination, as the handle is shot off. The reason why the museum cannot physically obtain the pistol is because it is impossible for his widow to transport it through Erez, one of the Israeli checkpoints encasing Gaza in an impenetrable siege for over ten years.[7]

Every time I visit the Yasser Arafat Museum, I wonder why the photo of Abu Jihad's pistol is exhibited, since the museum is an obvious site for claiming the death of a revolutionary era and setting the stage for the narrative of the present political regime: peaceful negotiations, security coordination, and political complicity with the Israeli settler colonial regime. The photo of Jihad's weapon posits an opposing narrative of the museum. Naturally, we all know that the museum (and any other conduit for hegemonic ideology, for that matter) is not omniscient and that it leaks, breaks, and falters. However, this looks like a very deliberate curatorial decision. A photo of the pistol behind museum glass. I would postulate that it is an attempt at defunctionalizing the pistol, even while it is outside the museum. The museum would like to capture both militant past and present and put them to their death; thus, it situates resistance to settler colonialism in the past in an attempt to frame everything in a postcolonial time. The photograph of the pistol therefore carries within it the contradiction and tension within this museum.

However, contrary to the desire of the museum, the photo of the pistol has invoked various stories, rumours, and myths as to why the pistol is missing. In fact, the photo looks like a wanted poster. The museum wishes to capture the fugitive pistol, but as sometimes happens with wanted posters, its purpose backfires, transforming the outlaw into a popular figure of rebellion. In *The Undercommons*, Stefano Harney and Fred Moten write of the fugitive as the outlaw, as the rebel, the one who stands their ground against the settlers.[8] Evading the relationship between the powerful and powerless, the fugitive is rather the one who transgresses this relationship of binaries by refusing 'to be corrected'.[9] Similarly, some objects are compelled by colonial powers to refuse to enter the museum, to refuse to be transformed into pure postcolonial form, into corpses of colonial time.

Take Three: The Museum Before or After the Revolution?

As stated above, the Louvre is considered by many to mark the birth of the modern museum. The conversion of the palace into a museum was propelled by the French Revolution. As discussed by Boris Groys, the decision by the revolutionaries whether to destroy the palace or not was resolved by converting it into a museum, an iconoclastic response which turns everything in the museum into material evidence of the death of the past regime(s).[10] This irrevocable death marks a new political era outside the museum, de-functionalizing its objects, transforming them into art.[11] So, the museum's time, according to Groys, is after the end of a revolution. The museum in this way functions to deem not only what is inside of it irrevocably dead but also the revolution itself. Revolutions are defined by the present, as they are usually the moment of destruction of the present regime. Once this regime is destroyed, the revolution is destroyed along with it. Museums are built to commemorate those revolutions; they become both evidence of the death of a past regime and guarantor that another revolution is unnecessary. This is precisely the case with the Yasser Arafat Museum; it commemorates the history of the militant era, or what Palestinians refer to as the Palestinian Revolution, subsequently hurling it into the past. With the post-revolutionary museum in place, there is no longer a reason to revolt. Time in the modernist museum moves between history and the future. The present is only a tunnel. History is employed to determine the future, and the future is rather posited as the present.

Take Four: The Secret

There is another notorious gun in the Palestinian imagination. During the—continuing—Nakba of 1948, many Palestinians buried their valuable belongings (ranging from photos to gold) in their backyards or secret locations, so they would be able to retrieve them once they return, not knowing that many of them will remain buried for decades. However, the stories of those underground remainders keep circulating in the diaspora and across generations. In the satirical novel *The Secret Life of Saeed: The Pessoptimist* by Emile Habibi, there is such a story. The novel centres around the strange time of the Nakba aftermath. Chronicling the struggles and transformations of the antihero, Saeed, and his family, the story spans two generations, wherein his son is empowered by the buried objects. Two secrets haunt the novel: the first is that Saeed is a collaborator with the new regime, and the second is a buried treasure box that his wife's family hid in a cave in their village, Tantoura, before they were forcibly expelled in 1948. Eventually, their son finds the treasure box, which contains guns and gold, and becomes a *Fida'i* (resistance fighter).

The Nakba of 1948 defined the Palestinians as a collective through the shared experience of death and expulsion. The moment of death and burial is simultaneously the moment of birth and reproduction.[12] Therefore, the novel's return to the buried treasure follows this form of movement. Throughout the novel, the buried treasure functions like a promise of salvation, a reminder of a possible return, the potential for some kind of emancipation. Indeed, the story of the treasure box enables the son to become a resistance fighter. The act of burial produces life; the stories of the buried objects circulate among the Palestinians, they are kept alive through continuous oral chronicling.

Take Five: What about the Present?

In 'All Shall Be Unicorns', Marina Vishmidt writes about the notion of the commons and art activism in relation to time. She juxtaposes communist time with commonist time. Vishmidt argues that the fulfilment of communism takes place after the revolution; thus, it exists in the future while commonist time takes place in the present. Commonism is rooted in the present because, instead of waiting for the future revolution or political mobilization against the state, or making demands of the state, it launches its affirmative projects in the here and now. In the modernist conception of time, and its association with progress, the present and the future become binaries, as we resist the present and work towards a 'better' future. According to Vishmidt, the commons is still 'future-oriented', but embodied rather than using time as a medium for its realization. The commons 'does not oppose the present but proposes an active reconstruction of it from within.'[13] Moreover, this idea of progress, which sees the present as the tunnel for the future, is at the very core of capitalism, as financial markets are based on future projections and speculation. Postponement and delay are tactics of the market and a means to control the present. According to Timothy Mitchell, even the construction of infrastructure is built to delay and accumulate interest and profit.[14] However, the future orientation of the solution to come is futile in the case of settler colonialism. For the oppressed, the present and the everyday are determined by struggle and resistance. Thus, a deferral into the future constitutes self-denial.[15]

Practices of the commons are also rooted in the everyday. Capitalism pervades every aspect of our lives—its violence is slow. Vishmidt discusses the different discourses of the left around the fight with capitalism, and a futurist orientation seems to pervade. Those discourses are set after the destruction of capitalist institutions opens the way for communist living. Commonism is instead situated in the present and is rather affirmative, building communities and support structures which are based on alternative economies, slowly and silently leaving those hegemonic institutions to falter and fall. So,

[redacted]

is the time of the museum in resistance the present?

The museum in struggle needs to be a site of burials. As Groys writes, contrary to the prevalent narrative of calling the museum a graveyard, the graveyard is a space full of possibilities.[16] Stories about graveyards abound. Death in the graveyard becomes generative. Spirits inhabit the present. In popular culture, there are many stories about corpses awakening at graveyards—less so at museums.[17] The secret and promise of finding the treasure box in *The Pessoptimist* functions in the same way. The buried treasure box reminds the son of his mother's village and the necessity for return. Similar to Abu Jihad's missing pistol, the story of the object and its emancipatory powers survives because of its lack of exposure.

Take Six: Archives in Resistance

The museum of resistance is a museum engaged in struggle. Therefore, it is a museum outside of time. During the first intifada in Palestine, underground communiqués were discarded by burial; they were deemed illegal by the Israeli military, and any Palestinian caught reading or in possession of one was arrested. So, the communiqués had to disappear after they were read. Burning was not an option, since the traces are incriminating, so it is said that they were dumped in wet concrete construction sites or buried underground. The future material exposure of these documents implicated their readers and authors. This is precisely the danger of the exhibition of a material archive during a struggle. Any record is incriminating. To be outside of time is to be outside the reaches of the archive and surveillance. It is through the collective practice of struggle and resistance that a community can attempt to be outside of time. It is through preserving a secret together.

The late 1980s in Palestine were distinguished by collective emancipatory knowledge production and radical imagination. Another form of an archive in resistance is a book named *Falsafat al Muwajahah Wara al Qudban*, or *The Philosophy of Confrontation Behind Bars*. This book was smuggled in fragments inside of capsules by political prisoners and circulated outside and inside of Israeli prisons to educate Palestinians about how to confront political imprisonment. The book does not contain any publishing information; neither the author, the publication date, nor printing information are mentioned. Scholar Esmail Nashif writes about the deliberate absence of this information:

> ***The main characteristic of the space/time of the no-naming practice is the fact of being out of reach of the colonizer's surveillance practices. But in the case of*** Philosophy of the Confrontation Behind Bars, ***this being out of reach is not a passive fragile insulation. On the contrary, the invisibility is capitalized on to resist the colonizer whose eye is blinded by the secrecy. The act of no-naming blinds the colonizer's eye/discourse.***[18]

The absence of the information places the book outside of a record of time and space which the colonizer controls. To achieve this resistance to the time and space of the colonizer, authorship should encompass the collective: 'The author is the collectivity... By not naming it, one reproduces the myth of the We.'[19] The record of knowledge by the Palestinian collective body was materialized and circulated because it was necessary to share in and for resistance. However, the way it was disseminated protected the collective instead of exposing it. The absence of a date places this body of knowledge outside of time, making it impossible to capture yet available to everyone. The underground authorship and circulation of collective knowledge is one of the aspects of a museum in resistance. The medium of this museum is continuous collective dissemination rather than a building made of concrete with an immovable collection about resistance.

Postscript (2025)

Six years since this text was written, the stakes of its arguments have only intensified. The genocide unfolding in Gaza today has made brutally clear what was always latent in this reflection: that Palestinian material and cultural archives remain under threat of constant erasure; centralizing them in museums while still under settler colonial rule will not save

[redacted]

them from destruction; and that the museum—in resistance—must remain fugitive, mobile, and alert to erasure.

In Gaza over the last twenty months, entire libraries, universities, historical monuments, and cultural centres have been systematically destroyed. Artists, poets, musicians, and educators are being targeted and killed. The bodies of knowledge they carried—often undocumented, oral, intergenerational—are at risk of annihilation. The destruction is not incidental; it is structural. It is epistemicide: the erasure of a people's capacity to narrate their own pasts and imagine their futures.

And yet, the stories persist. Through underground networks, voice notes, broken servers, fragments of poems transmitted on phones with no signal—Gaza resists archival death. The museum in resistance, in this moment, is not an institution but an encrypted message, a shared meal, a radio broadcast from beneath the rubble. It is not simply outside of time, but against the colonial control of time. It is no longer about remembering, but about refusing to forget on their terms. The fragmentation of the cultural archive has become its most robust archive. People all over the world today hold fragments of knowledge together.

To speak of museums, of curating, of archiving under these conditions demands not abstraction but action. It demands that we ask: What do we collect, and who does it protect? If documentation exposes the vulnerable, then secrecy is not absence—it is shelter. And when international art institutions remain silent, or 'neutral', they participate in the genocide of meaning.

Let us then, once again, think of the buried pistol, the missing archive, the oral myth—not as losses to recover, but as forms of resistance. Not everything must survive in the museum. Some things must survive *outside* of it, in defiance in order to persist. Today, as cultural workers, our task is not to preserve the past, but to ensure that the future cannot be built without accounting for this unbearable present.

Notes

1 • From the poem 'The Exiles Don't Look Back' by Mahmoud Darwish. See Mahmoud Darwish, *Now, As You Awaken*, trans. Omnia Amin and Rick London (San Francisco: Sardines Press, 2006).
2 • Hito Steyerl, 'A Tank on a Pedestal: Museums in an Age of Planetary Civil War', *e-flux*, no. 70 (February 2016), www.e-flux.com/journal/70/60543/a-tank-on-a-pedestal-museums-in-an-age-of-planetary-civil-war.
3 • Ibid.
4 • Ibid.
5 • Mahdi Amel, 'Al Thaqafa Wal Thawra', *Al Hiwar Al Mutamadden*, 23 May 2016, www.ahewar.org/debat/show.art.asp?
6 • Yasser Arafat, 'Yasser Arafat's 1974 UN General Assembly speech', United Nations General Assembly, New York, 13 November 1974.
7 • In the larger context of the PA, the Palestinian police cannot even move with their weapons between different zones and ghettos, as connecting roads are under Israeli control.
8 • Stefano Harney and Fred Moten, *The Undercommons: Fugitive Planning & Black Study* (New York: Minor Compositions, 2013).
9 • Ibid, p. 1.
10 • Boris Groys, 'On Art Activism', *e-flux*, no. 56 (2014): pp. 1–14.
11 • Groys even suggests that it is the modernist museum which marks the transformation of design into art.
12 • Esmail Nashif, *Images of a Palestinian's Death* (Beirut: Arab Center for Research and Policy Studies, 2015).
13 • Marina Vishmidt, 'All Shall Be Unicorns: About Commons, Aesthetics and Time', *Open! Platform for Culture, Art & The Public Domain*, 3 September 2014, www.onlineopen.org/download.php?id=128.
14 • Timothy Mitchell, 'Infrastructures Work on Time', *e-flux architecture* (28 January 2020), www.e-flux.com/architecture/new-silk-roads/312596/infrastructures-work-on-time.
15 • Joseph Massad uses the term postcolonial colony to describe Palestine, with which he presents a historical argument where Zionism presents Israel as a postcolony. See Joseph A. Massad, *The Persistence of the Palestinian Question: Essays on Zionism and the Palestinians* (New York. Routledge, 2006).
16 • Groys, 'On Art Activism'.
17 • Ibid.
18 • Esmail Nashif, *Palestinian Political Prisoners: Identity and Community* (New York: Routledge, 2008).
19 • Ibid.

[redacted]

Walid Taher, *They Humiliated, Belittled, Impoverished, Silenced Me and Made Me Disbelieve in the Divine, They Categorized, Hurt and Blew Me Up. I Exploded, I Won, I Was Happy, I Flew, Now It's Your Turn to Join Me*, 2011

بهدلوني... صغّروني.. فقّرون

كفّروني.. صنّفوني.. عوّروني..

إنفجرت.. إنتصرت.. فرحت

Part 3
Grief

The Art of Loss and Mourning

[redacted]

To Break Up with I'

Naama Shoshana
Fogiel Lewin

Dear I'

We were in a relationship for twenty-two years. We grew up together. I remember I loved you. Your beauty, your poetry, your warmth, your touch will remain forever an invisible tattoo on my skin. I am breaking up with you in English, so Hebrew will stay mine. I remember I was a Zionist. You asked me repetitively to remember. You played with my memory, so I will remember to love you. I was learning to draw your body. Learning to act, believe, and be what you ask for.

Now cry. Now smile. Celebrate. Remember. Make a mess. Be organized. Be sad. Be happy. People die for us to be alive. Be proud we are Israelis. Be proud we are Jewish. We lost. We are winning. We are the victims. We are the chosen ones. They hate us. We are marvels. They want to kill us. We survived. We will live forever. Be scared for your life. Never forget what they did to us. Live in fear. Be confident. Do not apologize. They should apologize. Run away. Hide. Stay here forever. Do not leave this place, ever. Here is the only safe place for Jews. Go outside to the world. Make us proud. Prove to the world they were wrong. Make them sorry. We are the best. We are the chosen ones. We are the trauma. We are heroes. We are in pain. We are safe. We are in danger.

You never allow anyone to question you, not sincerely. Most of your nation never questions you. The fact that Jewish people can be victims does not mean we do not have a responsibility when power arrives in our hands. You are declaring yourself as the state of the Jewish people. But you are truly the state of Jewish exclusivity and supremacy. Judaism is not Zionism.

The process of creating you integrated into reality a specific manner of colonialism, as the Zionist movement had learned from European colonialism. You should have already understood that there is no safety in colonizing, occupying, and controlling, and that there is no peace in genocide.

Your biggest lies are about you providing safety. You never do so. Never fully take into account the people you kill. Israelis and Palestinians.

And many more. To be able to live in you, I had to accept violence, war, and trauma as a regular thing. I had to accept that you cannot do your part in the state-citizen agreement regarding safety. I failed to do so.

I knew I did not want to serve in the army when I was nine years old. On the first selection day I attended, I shared with the soldier who checked my data my fear of weapons. I hoped she would send me to an army psychiatrist, who would understand I could not serve and would let me out. She did not send me there, and the day selection continued.

The months before my due date for starting my two years of service were about finding my way out. I got a letter from an old therapist saying I would be unable to survive mentally and physically in a militarist service. I was crying on phone calls with the army, faking panic attacks, and requesting to meet an army psychiatrist before my recruitment day. I cried in the waiting room before my meeting. Wearing a big sweater, even though it was thirty degrees Celsius, so my body would look smaller. Holding a plastic glass of water that an eighteen-year-old soldier gave me. I cried during the meeting with the psychiatrist. She promised me she would let me out the moment I entered the door, and yet I kept avoiding her eye contact as was recommended to me. I called my mom after the meeting, crying, while waiting for the psychiatrist to sign my release papers from military service. I was sure I must be so mentally unstable if she let me out. I cried my way out of the army. You made me believe that if I found my way out of the army, there must be something wrong with me. It took me time to remember that you are the wrong one.

When I chose not to serve in your army, I knew I would never entirely belong to you. I was one thing—Israeli—but I was doing something else.

I try never to judge soldiers for being a soldier in you. I grew up in you, I remember how radical my action of 'crying myself out of the army' was seen. I remember friends I lost due to that. I remember the amount of militarist culture we were educated in as kids.

One moment they finish high school, the next they have a gun and are becoming objects, properties of the nation. They get to be part of the significant structure that collects you together. In a society and nation that sanctifies the army, to be a soldier is always to be a hero, and to refuse to take part in the militaristic culture is a betrayal. You send people to die for you. In the name of protection, in the name of history, in the name of love.

[redacted]

During my last year of high school, my classmates' favourite conversation subject was 'Who will die in the army?' Who will be the one to sacrifice their life for you to continue to be alive? It was probably a way to release the growing tension. They grew up in you. They knew and heard about soldiers who died, were kidnapped, and put in prison for you. They knew that you would keep creating wars, which now will be their turn to fight. The fear of dying for you was confirmed and validated by the reality and the narrative surrounding it. With it, it could not be exposed as a fear, only as a joke.

By joining the army, the land upon which you are living becomes a motherland to the people who claim it, grab it, and die on it. Taking territory, space, and nature from another population, appropriating the land as their belonging. You try to intervene in the memory of the land and to jump from Biblical times to current ones, ignoring all the lives that have happened in the middle. The land was never empty.

Lands are never empty, and they also do not belong to anyone. If anything, we belong to a land. I belong between the river and the sea.

You are a bully, both to Israelis and to Palestinians. You never give a fuck about people who die and suffer and are traumatized because of you. You never count Palestine and the Arab world as equals to you; by that, their death is not equal. They are numbers, that is all.

You are pushing and playing with emotional buttons, then acting innocent. You are abusive. I remember everything you did, all the wars and almost-war moments. I remember all the times you tried to look innocent but made clear choices of disrespect, emotional violence, and physical violence. You are a delusion of care.

I remember the first war I experienced when I started to understand it.

Alarm.

You taught me that if I hear the alarm sounds, I need to hide and run away. So I did. The moment I chose to leave you was at the end of one 'what to do in case of a war' practice in school. It was the first day of school after the summer of 2006. As it is in many other schools, the shelter in our school was also the art room. We sat on the floor between the big tables, next to scissors, coloured papers, pencils, gouache paints, brushes, and more art supplies. Waiting until one of the adults says the war practice is over and we can get our ten o'clock break. *I was ten years old. I went crying to the principal's office. I told her I wished I lived in France, like my cousins and other family members. Saying I wish to leave you.*

A', the principal of the school, looked at me. She tried to tell me that it is not better there, and that also in France there is violence and, even more frighteningly, anti-Semitism.

It did not matter to me. They don't kill each other, I was thinking.

The choreographies you create will be stuck in my body forever as an uncontrollable reaction. The traumas will keep living in my body, creating Homeland Allergies. There are so many more movement options, internal and external, to a land, and a body. There are so many options for being besides the one you taught me. I used to be you. I left you. Now I am breaking up with you. Now, I am a continuous action of separation.

Bye I'

N'

[redacted]

Grief and Healing amid a Genocide

Roschanack Shaery-Yazdi

Tragic events, counterintuitively perhaps, have a way of sometimes healing our deepest wounds. By healing, I refer to the act when the merciless fingers of grief scratch open frantically in a trance, ancient scars as if they had received some cosmic hint that there lay a hidden treasure. In that moment, we don't spin in our rational mind, wondering how much courage we have; instead, this wild force of pain opens a long-forgotten pathway and forces truth to blur out. Initially, that truth has a squeaky voice! That kind of fierce grace, the bottomless grief, breaks all barriers; it is not her job to do the usual cost-benefit calculations. It wants expression. Grief is the older sibling of courage. It sometimes just bullies courage out of its cozy corner.

The grief of witnessing the ongoing genocide in Gaza dug so meticulously yet so abruptly inside my being that it spat out something I could only later, on examination under a microscope, identify as my inner whiteness. In less poetic language, one may compare the process to our attempt to get some ketchup from a glass ketchup bottle. We hit the bottom of the glass, and nothing happens. We hit a second, a third time, and suddenly, to our surprise and frustration, the entire bottle is emptied on our plate. The genocide was that last hit, when one fall day, my whole inner whiteness was unceremoniously spewed out of my middle-aged body onto a random street in a random European city. This internalized whiteness had sat so comfortably like a parasite in my nervous system, camouflaging and shapeshifting, that I had no idea it even existed. It seems I had inherited it from my ancestors: I was thinking their thoughts, continuing their legacies and beliefs. The parasite had disguised itself entirely as me, not just as part of me, but as my entire identity. It took a genocide to wake me up from dreaming other people's dreams and from protecting other people's privileges.

Waking Up to the Other Within Me

Don't get me wrong, I have gone through tragic events before. I was born in the early 1970s in Germany to Iranian parents who diligently focused on upward mobility. When we returned to Iran a few years before the Iranian Revolution, my older sister and I were sent to a German international school in Tehran to safeguard the family's image of modernity and secularism. There, among German children whose parents worked in Iran and among half-Iranian children, we full-blooded Iranians with our thick black hair and darker skin stood out as the extras, the out-of-place people. If, in our culture, touching and hugging friends were the norm, the disgust in the eyes of our German teacher and the fellow German students when we Iranians laughed loudly and chased each other on the playground made us feel like showing emotions was proof of our backwardness. We therefore ran the danger of sliding down the class strata, for it was class that compensated for our darker skins and made the German teachers bear our 'lack of manners'. Their eyes spoke: '*Keine Emotionen, bitte!*' (No emotions, please!), as if showing emotions was as bad as coming to school with dirty clothes or falling asleep during class. The sad part was that the entire milieu I grew up in supported the idea that controlling emotions as successfully as the next-door white kid did, would also fill our piggy bank towards the end goal of being recognized as upper class. I, ambitious as I was, even back then as a child, and with a family whose discipline and work ethic were legendary, wanted to be a living example of a white child. I could not let my family down by holding loosely the rope to salvation. The chronic psychological abuse of disciplining us to behave white (whatever that construct meant in the 1970s in Iran) was not the main tragic event in my life.

A revolution, a war, forced migrations, divorces, chronic depression, and the untimely death of close family members each time forced me to let go of something I thought was dear to my heart and was part of what defined me as a human being. Like most other Third World displaced, the legendary clutches of 'events' followed me like a shadow. Despite all this, watching the genocide of the Palestinians unfold while living in Europe among those who were either indifferent, sceptical, or supportive of the Israeli perpetrators was an entirely different type of suffering. In the initial phases of the genocide, it had the effect of feeling a sense of disintegration, annihilation, pushed not just to the edge of a cliff but way beyond it, directly into the abyss. When,

[redacted]

in a public interview, a Holocaust survivor and supporter of the Palestinian cause explained that she would feel thirsty the entire day after Israel had cut off the water in Gaza, I felt a sense of relief knowing that I am not pretending the intensity of the effect the genocide had on me. I could not trust my emotions to be authentic, mainly because the aloof behaviour of most colleagues I worked with proved to the inner whiteness that I was indeed being 'unnecessarily dramatic'. It kept whispering: 'Keep it together, and don't throw tantrums.'

Within a month of the genocide, grief brought a chair, forced me to sit, and began asking uncomfortable questions: Who are you? *Who are you really?* Where are you from? *Where are you really from?* What do you believe? *What do you really believe?* From one to ten, where do you stand with your courage? Who are your friends? *Who are your friends, really?* Where are you going? *Where are you really going?*

Who really knows the answers to these difficult questions? But this grief wasn't in the mood to let me slip away. It was looking straight into my soul, asking me to fall apart right then and right there and have faith that I will one day have the energy to pick up the pieces of myself and reconstruct something new. I had no such faith, no such energy, no such optimism. Little did I know back then that what I was letting go of—in some parallel universe without colonialism—was not part of me to begin with.

I avoided looking grief directly in the eyes, ashamed because I could see the reflections of my cowardice. I wanted this whole violence to end so that *I* did not have to answer those questions that made me so utterly uncomfortable. I knew the genocide in Gaza was the beginning of a new world order, and with it, a new internal world order for me. I wanted to cheat, pretend that I could somehow be exempt from this exam. I was used to coexisting with violence: in my position as a professor at a university in Europe, I wanted to be seen as rational, as someone who could speak in a calm voice, even if witnessing the worst atrocities, as someone who could share a seat with perpetrators and those enablers who cheered them up with their silence. My internalized whiteness was not just genderless, it was a bad-ass privileged old-style colonialist white man who feared nothing more than being associated with my actual me: a brown woman from the Third World who through a combination of arduous work and divine grace had made it to a position of power. Oh, maybe I am mixing up the voices; in *his* eyes, it was only a divine prank that had brought me to the position of power. Worst of all, the old white man would shriek at what he heard as my squeaky voice when he thought this brown woman was getting all 'theatrical' and 'paranoid' about white supremacy, seeing things and making connections that, in his eyes, I was making up and exaggerating.

By the middle of 2024, I didn't know that a tomorrow could exist, not to speak of one day taking pride in this brown woman that was now determined to kick this senile white man out of her life. For the months to come, there was just pain, anger, rage, futile arguing with colleagues, hopelessness, occupation of the university space, more futile debates with the university administration, hatred, disbelief, frustration, petition writing, and finally, total exhaustion. Then, tired of the repetition: silence... and finally, self-blame. I had run out of moves to generate any meaningful change to contribute to holding Israel accountable for its atrocities.

Goodbye 'Good Migrant'

Just then, GRIEF came to visit again. This time, more compassionate, calmer, it said: 'Decolonizing Palestine is also about decolonizing the self; it is about tuning down the voice of self-blame and redirecting that blame where it belongs: to white supremacists and Israeli colonialists.' The mission to liberate Palestine was asking each one of us to become epic warriors, as there was no time for doubt and internal struggles anymore. Perhaps I could hear that message because the inner whiteness had packed and hit the road, and in the power vacuum created, an old, wise Iranian granny had rushed in and taken a seat on a flowery Persian carpet. Within months of her presence, I developed a superpower: I could hear and see gaslighting as it was happening, and I was not acting like a bastard child of an Iranian and a

[redacted]

European anymore, standing between two parents trying to make peace between them. I was done with the invisible and unpaid emotional labour of a cultural translator and said goodbye to my day job as a 'good migrant'. Israel's brutal extermination of an entire Palestinian life with the support of the United States and European governments and institutions taught me to grow up and know my place. My place was not to please narcissistic Europeans and clap when they performed their favourite activity: throwing tantrums when the world set boundaries for them and did not praise them for destroying the planet. Neither was I going to run into the arms of my fellow nationalists and flip the coin to take as face value the glorious stories about 2,500 years of history of my country of origin. My job was to develop my own voice. What follows is a teaser of what I can only imagine will be a much louder voice soon, finally joining the crowd of those healed creators who have seen this all along.

It's Not Me, It's You

To the privileged white/right Europe:

I am NOT part of you, I have no plans to be included in your nationalism, I do not have to carry your so-called historical responsibilities, I am not a descendant of colonialists, my ancestors did not get wealthy by exploiting other countries, my history thankfully does not share your so called enlightenment turn, I am therefore not delusional. Now that I have healed from the big fat parasite inside me, I finally see clearly and I do not believe a word that comes out of your mouth. A year and a half into the genocide, when someone asks me where I come from, I say I am Iranian, but unfortunately I live in the diaspora in Europe. I do not live here voluntarily, I did not take refuge in Europe; Europe and your support of US policies displaced me and millions like me. It is not us living off your wealth, it is you living off our wealth. In the name of a free-market economy and promoting democracy, your factories produce parts for weapons, your ports are open to carry them around the world, and you support authoritarian regimes so you can dump your garbage in our countries and receive cheap natural resources. Our misery, our people who collect the trash, drive trucks that bring food to your supermarkets, clean the hospitals and schools, those who carry out all the dirty work that remains invisible to you because they do it quietly day in day out, those overqualified migrants who work in mediocre jobs, all of them allow you to enjoy your 'free time' biking and hiking. Don't tell me you are not responsible for what your ancestors did, because colonialism has not yet ended and you are still participating in it. We are all part of genealogies and lineages; you are not exempt from that logic. You will never recognize the truth, so I will not waste my time fighting you. Your days are numbered, because you are already outnumbered. Instead, I will join the voices of those who also resist you.

To the privileged white/left Europe:

Let us clarify our boundaries and then start anew. Let us say goodbye and grieve our separation so we can greet each other with fresh eyes and a clear mind. Let us stand on our own feet, no longer hiding behind each other. We each come with our burdened histories, ancestral traumas, and dramas. It is your duty to educate your people; it is our duty to defend our rights. Please do not appropriate our symbols; use your own in your movement for liberation. We form alliances, but we are not perfectly parallel mirrors. Your cause is different than mine, you are still enjoying the white privilege and have not been displaced. You did not lose friends and family members in wars; you are not aging in diaspora with an incoherent life narrative. You must speak of the nuances of white privilege, but not to us; we already know that. You must gather your courage to talk to a different audience that goes deaf when you appropriate our symbols. Dig into your own history, find your own heroes and motivating stories. No, it is not phony to do that. Herewith, I issue a permission slip for you to develop compelling stories based on your history and culture that may bridge the gap between you and the white supremacist.

You must also grieve, just as we do daily. Grief purifies, grief gives courage, grief gives direction, grief wants the truth. When we have all grieved enough—perhaps one day—we can

[redacted]

realize that dream where race is not separating our experiences anymore. But for that utopia to become a reality, you must go to the lion's den and test your limits. I no longer give you refuge and hide you behind my back. I will not clap any longer for your performance to speak to me about white privilege. The path to true coexistence also goes through your emotional and intellectual labour: grieve, go out there, and have courage!

Glossary of Terms

Inner whiteness

- Allowing the privileged white to gaslight you and cast doubt about what you see and know based on the fact that historically your ancestors believed in the superiority of the white man
- Remaining silent and seated, thereby contributing to the reproduction of white supremacy
- 'Acting rational' and 'engaging in dialogue', even though you know these are buzzwords to keep us subjugated
- Believing anger and rage are an inappropriate response despite all the blatant abuse and oppression
- Acting upbeat in front of racist white people to prove you are 'emotionally balanced' despite their systemic support of atrocities around the world
- Bypassing courage and allowing oppression in the name of forgiveness and understanding

Grief

- Remembering you once belonged
- Believing when you hear them say you do not belong in Europe
- Parting paths
- The pain of the loss of innocence
- The pain of growth

Courage

- The ability to grieve the loss of your homeland, the loss of your friends and family
- The act of accepting that to belong, you must speak up

- Practicing seeing clearly
- Changing vocabulary, ending the reproduction of the perpetrator's language

Coexistence

- No colour-blindness
- Not needing to hide behind the left
- Not giving a refuge to the left
- Going beyond anger and demands only when structures change, and not a second earlier
- LOVE: forgiveness in light of actual compensation and considerate structural justice

Manual: Replacing Inner Whiteness with an Epic Warrior

ON

Disbelief, anger, mobilization, hopelessness, rage, exhaustion, more rage, more disbelief, more mobilization, burnout, burnout, collapse

OFF

Darkness, confusion, disorientation

ON

Grief-grief-grief... *Weltschmerz*

OFF

Cynicism, impatience, self-
blaming

(The big jump)

ON

An Epic Warrior

(Repeat cycle as often as needed)

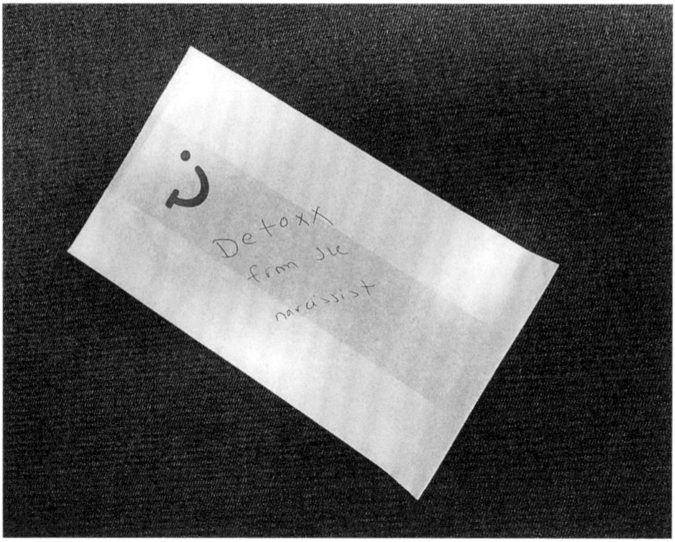

Roschanack Shaery-Yazdi, *Decolonize: Throw Up Your Inner Whiteness*, photograph

Free Permission Coupons to Decolonize

- You have the right to protest
- You have the right to make others uncomfortable
- You have the right to tell the truth
- You have the right to insist that there is a truth out there
- You have the right to get an allergic reaction to the following phrases: dialogue, two narratives, objectivity, rational, slow process, reviewing, neutrality...
- You have the right to be angry
- You have the right to disconnect from racist, sexist people
- You have the right to refuse to care for the fragility of white settlers and their cohorts
- You have the right to repeat yourself over and over
- You have the right to polarize
- You have the right to carry a puke bag to detox and to relieve yourself directly in front of the perpetrators when they attempt to gaslight, breadcrumb, or lecture you about human rights values and the importance of pluralism

[redacted]

When There Is No Body to Grieve For

Lara García Diaz

Grief is often understood as an intense emotional response to loss, but as Roland Barthes powerfully illustrates in his *Mourning Diary* (2010), it is also a prolonged, unresolved process that challenges the very limits of language. Following the death of his mother, Barthes turns to writing as a way of confronting the inexpressibility of loss, revealing how language, though inadequate, can nonetheless sustain a fragile bond with the absent. For Barthes, the irreversibility of death renders the lost subject irreplaceable, and it is precisely this permanence that makes mourning resist closure. Through daily reflection, he unveils mourning as a lingering wound: an open-ended journey where language falters yet becomes the fragile thread that binds us to what has been lost.

In Barthes, however, the possibility of inhabiting mourning is closely tied to the presence of a body whose absence can be named, recognized, and processed. But how can mourning be theorized when there is no body—when absence remains unresolved, and the material evidence of loss is missing? This question becomes especially urgent in the context of Spain's recent history. During the Spanish Civil War (1936–1939) and the Francoist dictatorship that followed (1939–1975), the state was responsible for widespread human rights violations: enforced disappearances, extrajudicial executions, torture, and systematic persecution based on political, religious, sexual, and racial grounds. These crimes often involved not only the erasure of lives, but the erasure of bodies themselves, denying families the possibility of closure, burial, or conventional mourning.

One of those vanished bodies was my grandfather's brother, whose presence reached me only through a single, time-worn photograph my grandfather kept tucked away in a drawer, as if protecting it from the world, or perhaps from memory itself. In our family, we never learned the whereabouts of my great-uncle's disappeared body; its absence lingered not only physically, but within the silences that followed. After my grandparents passed, the photograph, too, vanished into oblivion, leaving behind not just the faint memory of his image but the quiet discomfort it once provoked. That discomfort, that silence, became inseparable from the legacy of disappearance.

The Memorial Movement

The absence of a centralized and updated registry of victims and mass graves has severely impeded the implementation of a coordinated state policy aimed at the exhumation and identification of the remains of the disappeared.[1] In these contexts, the lack of a recoverable body displaces the mourning process for the families of the victims beyond the realm of symbolic processing of loss. It becomes a grief suspended in time—a 'frozen' mourning[2]—or one that persists in a state of deferred resolution, akin to what Pauline Boss (2001) defines as 'ambiguous loss'. For Boss, ambiguous loss is not predicated on the confirmation of death or the presence of a dead body, but on the radical uncertainty that surrounds the disappearance of a subject. This indeterminacy prevents the enactment of funerary rituals which, within Western cultural frameworks, are seen as necessary to inscribe loss within the register of 'the Real' and to enable a process of closure.[3] While Boss grounds her theoretical framework in examples such as the families of missing soldiers or caregivers of Alzheimer's patients, of relevance for me here is her insistence on the vital role of symbolic forms of recognition and restitution for those left to endure the unresolved absence.

Despite the enactment of the Historical Memory Law in 2007, as well as various regional regulations adopted in subsequent years, the Spanish state still fails to fully comply with its international obligations and has largely disregarded the recommendations issued by international human rights mechanisms in matters of truth, justice, reparation, and guarantees of non-repetition.[4] Drawing on data compiled by law scholar Elisenda Calvet Martínez, and based on the map of mass graves developed by the Spanish Ministry of Justice in 2011, a total of 4,265 graves had been officially recorded by 2021, corresponding to 57,911 documented victims.[5] Nonetheless, estimates at the time suggested that the number of disappeared persons could be as high as 100,000.

As historian Francisco Espinosa Maestre has argued, many deaths were never formally recorded, swallowed by the

[redacted]

pervasive climate of fear, leaving lives that were 'known by all but seen by none'.[6] Such was the fate of my grandfather's brother, whose presence lingers only in the quiet spaces of memory, a name whispered but never fully acknowledged, lost to time and silence. This absence, as anthropologist Jorge Moreno Andrés reflects, echoes through the domestic landscapes of the post–Civil War era, where homes became haunted by the empty places left by those who vanished: 'Homes in which someone was always missing; a loved one whose name was never mentioned outside the household.'[7] These silenced griefs, hidden in plain sight, often remain unspoken, only surfacing when shared and made intelligible through collective narration.

It is important to note that although the Francoist regime officially ended in 1975 and the democratic transition was subsequently implemented in Spain, it was not until the opening of the grave at Priaranza del Bierzo, in the province of León in the Autonomous Community of Castile-La Mancha, in the year 2000, that the exhumation of victims of Francoist repression began to be carried out with a degree of scientific rigour under the supervision of state authorities. This marked the beginning of what is now referred to as the Memorial Movement, led by the *Asociación para la Recuperación de la Memoria Histórica* (Association for the Recovery of Historical Memory, ARMH). Since then, this Memorial Movement has come to represent a mode of historical engagement that, as Walter Benjamin proposed in *On the Concept of History* (1940), brushes history 'against the grain', invoking that with which the Spanish state still struggles, and in many cases, refuses to acknowledge.

Designed 'To Count but Not to Search'

The role and sustained pressure of Spain's Memorial Movement have been essential in addressing the long-standing uncertainty surrounding the fate of those who disappeared between 1936 and 1975, including, as mentioned, my great-uncle. Far from being a merely symbolic initiative, this movement, and particularly through the work of the ARMH, has engaged in strategic legal and political advocacy to compel the Spanish state to address its historical obligations. Drawing on legal expertise from practitioners involved in cases of enforced disappearance in Latin America, the ARMH brought the Spanish case before the United Nations High Commissioner for Human Rights. Whereas exhumations of mass graves had previously been carried out exclusively by victims' families, the ARMH began to provide legal, logistical, and scientific support, thus institutionalizing a process that had long relied on grassroots efforts.

In that sense, although the Spanish Ministry of Justice created a national map of mass graves, critical voices have since pointed out the limitations of this initiative. As contributors to geoactivismo.org argue, this official registry risks reproducing the same bureaucratic and depoliticized logic it ostensibly seeks to challenge. In this regard, parallels can be drawn with other state-driven initiatives, such as Mexico's *Registro Nacional de Personas Desaparecidas y No Localizadas* (National Register of Disappeared and Missing Persons), which similarly positions itself as a tool of public accountability while often falling short of its mandate. Journalist Efraín Tzuc highlights how Mexico's national registry has largely failed to fulfil its stated goal of aiding in the identification and location of missing persons, functioning instead as what he describes 'as an opaque, incomplete, and bureaucratic marker—riddled with political opportunism, data manipulation, and ambiguous criteria—that renders official the number of disappeared persons, which has now surpassed 100,000.'[8] For Tzuc, Mexico's National Register legitimizes official figures while obscuring the lived realities behind them. Its main effect, he suggests, has been to stabilize the discourse on disappearance through official numbers, while masking political inaction and the structural violence that underlies these absences. This insight invites questioning, as contributors to geoactivismo.org suggest, the extent to which documentation alone, absent genuine political will, can serve the goals of truth, justice, or reparation.

The dynamics traced above reveal a stark contrast between, on the one hand, the bureaucratic and often symbolic gestures of the Spanish state and, on the other, the embodied,

[redacted]

politically committed practices of civil society organizations like the ARMH. As previously noted, the public exhumation of mass graves did not emerge from institutional initiative but rather from grassroots efforts that challenged the silence surrounding historical violence. The state's reliance on data collection echoes a broader logic of deferral and abstraction, in which the imperative to provide justice is displaced by administrative performances of concern. In contrast, the ARMH enacts what I might refer to here as a counter-archive: a form of memory work grounded in the intimate trauma of families and communities, and in the forensic evidence of violence that official narratives have long sought to obscure. As Salazar et al. observe, in the context of post-conflict Colombia, the partial and fragmented state responses constitute a form of 'non-integrated and incomplete reparation'.[9] In the case of my great-uncle, the restoration of a narrative obscured by silence and fear cannot be captured by mere numbers. This is a disappearance that defies any attempt to be quantified, for the body's whereabouts remain an unfathomable void, a space where even the most basic answers elude us.

Processes of Symbolic Reparation

Although the discourse has often been dominated by the symbolic and legal significance of exhumations, scholar Daniel Palacios González argues that during the 1970s and 1980s, clandestine, activist, and grassroots actions surrounding mass graves already served as meaningful forms of engagement for the relatives of victims. These early practices, though largely unofficial, facilitated processes of adaptation to loss and mourning within affected communities. As he explains, 'The memorial practice carried out during those years is replete with political signifiers that speak to the ethical dimension of those murdered. These were groups of people who began to gather informally yet shared a common objective: the preservation of memory.'[10] While exhumations undoubtedly represent a turning point in the processes of symbolic reparation, they should not be understood as the exclusive means through which bereaved families have articulated grief and demanded recognition. The creation of personal rituals and symbolic funerals, for instance, constitute alternative and powerful mechanisms for materializing memory and processing loss outside formal institutional frameworks.[11] A process 'in which memory gradually externalized beyond the mind to take on material forms. First, during the dictatorship, in an ephemeral fashion: stones, floral offerings. Later, in a more permanent manner: gardens, sculptures, monoliths placed over the graves containing the bodies, or mausoleums housing the exhumed remains.'[12]

These examples prompt Palacios González to reflect on the potential for the mass grave, once a symbol of state violence and repression, to be re-signified through both formal and discursive strategies. Transformed from a locus of terror into a space of memory, the mass grave assumes new meaning within the communities affected by loss, making possible processes of mourning for those denied the presence of a body or a grave through which to articulate their grief. Drawing on philosopher Judith Butler's reflections on grievability, these ritual practices serve to reassert the value and dignity of lives historically denied public mourning.[13] By enabling the acknowledgment and collective grieving of those whose deaths were rendered socially invisible, such acts not only contest normative boundaries of mournability but also contribute to the reconstitution of community through the shared work of mourning and memory. 'Through the act of offering flowers,' Palacios González notes, 'families ensured that the location of the mass graves would not be forgotten during the years of the dictatorship. By the 1970s, this gave way to a new period of possibilities for social action.'[14]

Material Testimonies and the Aesthetics of Mourning

Building on previous reflections about the significance of symbolic rituals in the absence of formal mourning practices, it is important to consider the role of personal objects recovered during exhumations. On several occasions, the exhumation of mass graves has not resulted in the recovery of human remains. Nevertheless, in such instances, the interventions undertaken have often allowed for the retrieval of a substantial number of material traces, such as garments and personal belongings, associated with the bodies of Republican soldiers, members of the insurgent forces, and/or civilian victims. During the excavations conducted as part of the 2020–2022 Graves Plan in Catalonia, for example, at least 3,073 such items were recovered. These personal objects have served as powerful stand-ins for absent remains, offering families and communities material substitutes for mourning and remembrance in the face of irretrievable loss.

In contexts where the absence of a body and the deprivation of funeral rites prevail, the objects recovered from mass graves can take on profound symbolic significance in the elaboration of what anthropologist Laura Marina Panizo terms 'extraordinary mourning'.[15] Unlike 'pathological mourning', extraordinary mourning is characterized by its complex entanglement with disappearance, life, death, ambiguity, and torture. As previously discussed in relation to the notion of ambiguous loss—the type of loss defined not by the presence of a dead body but by the indeterminacy surrounding the subject's disappearance—extraordinary mourning arises in critical death situations such as war, conflict, or post-conflict scenarios involving torture. Panizo underscores the importance of understanding mourning in these cases not as a linear response to a singular traumatic event, but rather as a process shaped by the interrelation, overlapping, or independence of multiple traumatic experiences.[16] In this way, ambiguous loss in post-war contexts is frequently marked not only by the uncertainty surrounding the disappearance itself but also by the unresolved and traumatic suspicion that the missing individual may have been subjected to violence.[17] Thus, the experience of trauma stems not merely from the absence of closure, but from the haunting indeterminacy of both the loss and the potential brutality that may have accompanied it.

Building on this idea of unresolved trauma rooted in the uncertainty of both loss and violence, Panizo introduces the analytical concept of *Pena Raíz* (*Rooted Grief*) to describe the mourning experiences of relatives of the detained and disappeared, specifically in the context of Northern Chile under

Pinochet's dictatorship. *Pena Raíz* captures not only the emotional toll of loss but also its entanglement with the political and structural dimensions of state violence. As Panizo explains, the term refers to 'a state of sorrow that enables a creative labour of continuity, struggle, and care within the framework of relationships established between survivors and the disappeared under State Terrorism.'[18] For Panizo, mourning emerges not only as a deeply personal process but also as a contingent force for political mobilization and solidarity among survivors and relatives of the disappeared.

In this context, the objects recovered from mass graves can be interpreted as material vessels through which different temporalities and modes of forgetting are summoned and negotiated. These material remnants bear witness to historical moments deliberately obscured or erased by an authoritarian regime. In psychological theory, the concept of the 'linking object' refers to material items that symbolically stand in for the deceased, serving as mediators in the process of mourning and in managing the affective disorientation brought about by loss. In contexts marked by enforced disappearance and ambiguous loss, such objects are not only instrumental in enabling closure through ritual practices associated with *Pena Raíz* but also become central to the collective negotiation of grief's political and structural dimensions. As such, these objects support broader processes of social reintegration and political articulation, resonating with earlier reflections on Palacios González' work and Butler's conceptualization of grief as a space of ethical and political emergence.

Endowed with mnemonic significance, the personal belongings of the disappeared persist as quiet witnesses, resisting the erosive forces of temporal distance and collective amnesia; an endurance often materialized through the creation of domestic altars, carefully maintained by relatives and loved ones as intimate sites of memory and affect. In that sense, and beyond the domestic sphere, the mnemonic potential of these objects extends nowadays as well into the public and institutional domains through their incorporation into artistic practices, exhibitions, and site-specific interventions. Such

[redacted]

aesthetic and curatorial initiatives aim to amplify the collective resonance of absence, transforming personal belongings into artefacts of public memory. Through their preservation, archival treatment, and aesthetic framing, these objects are reinscribed with meaning, contributing to broader processes of memorialization and historical reparation.

Building on these aesthetic practices of preservation and collective memory, *Las Pequeñas Cosas* (Little Things, 2020) stands out as a powerful exhibition that foregrounds the emotional and historical weight carried by the personal belongings of the disappeared. Organized by the research project *Mapas de Memoria* (Memory Maps), the exhibition presented thousands of objects, documents, letters, and photographs collected over more than a decade of investigative work.[19] These humble objects stand not only as tangible remnants of personal loss but also as enduring markers of a collective memory systematically suppressed under Francoist rule. Thus, these objects operate on two levels: as embodiments of personal grief and as tangible affirmations of a repressed historical memory that slowly reclaims its presence within the public domain. In this sense, the exhibition opens a space not only for collective reflection on memory, violence, and trauma but also for those of us who, like me, have been distanced from these histories due to the passage of time and the absence of a concrete narrative. It offers an opportunity to reclaim the potential of remembering what once seemed unnameable. Just as *Las Pequeñas Cosas* transforms the previously inexpressible into an acknowledged loss and a recognized crime, this process of remembering allows us to reawaken recognition and meaning from within the gaps left by historical erasure. Through this act of remembering, we can metabolize loss, restore dignity to the silenced bodies, and engage in the ongoing work of mourning and justice. From this very process, this text takes shape, not merely as an account, but as an attempt to recover and give form to something lodged in my memory; something that remains uncountable and ineffable precisely because it was never fully closed or resolved.

Absent Bodies, Present Images

An alternative approach to the subjective processing of loss is offered by anthropologist Jorge Moreno Andrés. Drawing on extensive fieldwork and sustained engagement with victims' families, particularly in the case of those who disappeared during the Spanish Civil War and under Franco's regime, Moreno Andrés reflects on the intimate gestures of care through which relatives interacted with photographs of their disappeared loved ones, imbuing these images with presence in the face of an irreparable absence. This third form most closely mirrors the experience in my own family. In my grandfather's case, the image was not just a photograph of his brother; it became a tender reflection of the body lost. A fragile stand-in for one who could no longer be embraced, whose remains were never given rest, and whose absence haunted the silence of an endless, unresolved search. In this way, the photograph became an essential link to the absent, as described by Moreno Andrés: a tangible presence to which words could be directed, a material embodiment of the vanished.

The photograph my grandfather kept of his brother did not simply serve as a visual representation but as a material proxy for the absent body; a substitute for one who could neither be touched, properly mourned through burial, nor geographically located. As Moreno Andrés argues, images such as this acquire an ontological weight that transcends their documentary value, serving as mediating objects in the articulation of grief. They become sites of relational continuity, enabling a dialogical engagement with the disappeared and anchoring emotional bonds in the material world. As he poignantly notes, the photograph constitutes 'the only place where the face of the disappeared remains,' thereby becoming, paradoxically, 'the most alive object in the entire home.'[20]

In another of his works, *Camera Lucida* (1980), Barthes draws on Proust's *In Search of Lost Time* (1908–1922) to reflect on how memory, recollection, and mental imagery are conceived as mechanisms for resisting the threat of forgetting and death. For Barthes, however, it is photography rather than involuntary memory, as posited by Proust, that most directly

[redacted]

engages with the irreducible absence engendered by death. In his theorization, photographs emerge as mediums that bear the ontological imprint of mortality, inscribed with the spectral trace of the deceased. For Barthes, photographs function as a mechanism for the recuperation of loss. An act of temporal displacement that transcends the image's tautological function and instead opens a space intimately bound to memory, temporality, and death. Within this framework, the re-signification of photographs belonging to the disappeared, as explored by Moreno Andrés, echoes Barthes's conception of photography as a foundational and labyrinthine locus through which memory is both materialized and inhabited. This dynamic, as Jacques Derrida suggests in 'The Deaths of Roland Barthes', entails 'the return of the dead within the very structure of their image and the phenomenon of their image.'[21]

Both the objects recovered from mass graves and the photographs of the disappeared serve as material surrogates for absent bodies. They are sites onto which care and mourning can be redirected when the physical presence of the loved one is no longer available.[22] Through acts of 'iconic substitution', they effectively take on the role of a grave.[23] As art historian Horst Bredekamp notes, such images and objects allow 'the body to be fully present, even though it is no longer composed of living matter.'[24] Photographs thus become central to domestic altars, or circulate in and out of private space, increasingly incorporated, as noted earlier, into artistic and curatorial projects that extend their mnemonic and affective value beyond the intimate sphere.

Ultimately, the photograph of my great-uncle has disappeared, yet the intent to recover the history it once represented, marked by the pain of unresolved mourning, remains steadfast. The absence of the photograph does not signal the cessation of this search; on the contrary, it amplifies the enduring persistence of memory. This ongoing quest is not simply an archival undertaking but rather a profound exercise in critically reflecting on how we engage with the material remnants of the past. As anthropologist Moreno Andrés underscores, the real challenge before us is to preserve the emotional and historical bonds these objects carry; bonds that link them to the lives of those who once held them.[25]

The task that lies ahead is not merely archival, but a profoundly ethical and political undertaking; one that urges us to imagine tender, enduring ways of approaching traumatic memory. In many cases, as in my own, this memory is held in the grip of a 'frozen' mourning, suspended in time yet pulsing through the present, a fragile reckoning still unfolding, still resisted, and still shaping the world we inhabit.[26] In this sense, in another of his famous phrases, Benjamin wrote, 'To each generation is given a weak messianic power, a power on which the past has a claim.'[27] My engagement with the lost photograph of my great-uncle, then, does not merely pertain to a personal history; it becomes an ethical imperative, a confrontation with the unresolved trauma that insists upon our reckoning and demands to be acknowledged; a claim that cannot be settled cheaply.[28]

Notes

1 • Francisco Ferrándiz, *El pasado bajo tierra* (Barcelona: Anthropos, 2014).
2 • Julieta Arbizu, Claudio Cepeda, and Mariana Kantt, 'Duelo sin cuerpo. Experiencias con familiares de desaparecidos en el mar', IV *Congreso Internacional y VII Congreso nacional de Psicologia* 5, no. 7 (2020).
3 • Ibid.
4 • Amnistía Internacional, 'España: Poner fin al silencio y a la injusticia. La deuda pendiente con las víctimas de la Guerra Civil Española y del régimen franquista. Sección Española de Amnistía Internacional', https://doc.es.amnesty.org/ms-opac/permalink/1@000015400.
5 • The map of mass graves created by the Spanish Ministry of Justice can be consulted at: Ministerio de la Presidencia, Justicia y Relaciones con las Cortes. (n.d.). Mapa de fosas. Gobierno de España, www.mpr.gob.es/memoriademocratica/mapa-de-fosas/Paginas/buscadorfosas.aspx.
6 • Francisco Espinosa et al., *Morir, matar, sobrevivir: La violencia en la dictadura de Franco* (Barcelona: Booket, 2004), p. 104.
7 • Jorge Moreno Andrés, *El duelo revelado. La vida social de las fotografías familiares de las víctimas del franquismo* (Madrid: Consejo Superior de Investigaciones Científicas, 2018), p. 21.
8 • Efraín Tzuc, 'Contar para no buscar, la paradoja del registro de las desapariciones', *Adónde Van Los Desaparecidos*, 19 May 2022, https://adondevanlosdesaparecidos.org/2022/05/19/registro-contador-despariciones-mexico, p. 1.

[redacted]

9 • Andrade Salazar et al., *Memoria, violencia lineal y pena moral: narrativas de la masacre de Trujillo* (Medellín: Editorial Kavilando, 2019), p. 9.
10 • Daniel Palacios González, 'Memoria, ética y educación desde las fosas comunes: más allá del duelo y el monumento', in 'Debate: Comunidades de práctica y el futuro de la educación ilemata', eds. Marina Garcés and Antonio Casado da Rocha, *Revista Internacional de Éticas Aplicadas*, no. 33 (2020): pp. 135–146.
11 • See Palacios González, 'Memoria, ética y educación desde las fosa comunes'.
12 • Ibid., p. 368.
13 • See Judith Butler, *Precarious Life: The Power of Mourning and Violence* (London: Verso, 2004).
14 • Palacios González, 'Memoria, ética y educación desde las fosa comunes', p. 137.
15 • See Laura Marina Panizo, '"Qué pena me da la pena": duelo, pena y rituales de paso en familiares de desaparecidos de la dictadura de Pinochet (Chile)', *Disparidades. Revista de Antropología* 79, no. 2, e984 (2024): pp. 2–12.
16 • Panizo, 'Qué pena me da la pena', p. 6.
17 • See ibid.
18 • Ibid., p. 6.
19 • Mapas de Memoria is a CIEMEDH (International Center for Memory and Human Rights Studies) and UNED (National University of Distance Education) initiative that investigates historical memory through ethnographic work, honouring the disappeared and addressing silenced pasts. It seeks to dignify silenced lives and illuminate the relationship between memory, violence, and trauma.
20 • Moreno Andrés, El duelo revelado, p. 195.
21 • Jacques Derrida, *Cada vez única. El fin del mundo*, trans. Manuel Arranz (Valencia: Pre-Textos, 2005), p. 75.
22 • Moreno Andrés, *El duelo revelado.*
23 • Horst Bredekamp, *Teoría del acto icónico* (Madrid: Akal/ Estudios Visuales, 2017).
24 • Ibid., p. 133.
25 • See Moreno Andrés, *El duelo revelado.*
26 • See Arbizu et al., 'Duelo sin cuerpo'.
27 • Walter Benjamin, *Sobre el concepto de historia* (Madrid: Cuadrados, 2024), p. 17.
28 • Ibid.

References

• Amnistía Internacional. 'España: Poner fin al silencio y a la injusticia. La deuda pendiente con las víctimas de la Guerra Civil Española y del régimen franquista. Sección Española de Amnistía Internacional'. www.doc.es.amnesty.org/ms-opac/permalink/1@000015400.
• Arbizu, Julieta, Claudio Cepeda, and Mariana Kantt. 'Duelo

sin cuerpo. Experiencias con familiares de desaparecidos en el mar'. *IV Congreso Internacional y VII Congreso nacional de Psicologia* 5, no. 7 (2020): pp. 141–147.
• Barthes, Roland. *La cámara lúcida*. Trans. Joaquín Sala-Sanahuja. Barcelona: Paidós, 1989.
• Barthes, Roland. *Mourning Diary*. Trans. Richard Howard. New York: Hill and Wang, 2010.
• Benjamin, Walter. *Sobre el concepto de historia*. Madrid: 2Cuadrados, 2024. First published in 1940.
• Bredekamp, Horst. *Teoría del acto icónico*. Madrid: Akal/ Estudios Visuales, 2017.
• Butler, Judith. *Precarious Life: The Power of Mourning and Violence*. London: Verso, 2004.
• Da Silva Catela, Ludmilla. *No habrá flores en la Tumba del pasado. La experiencia de reconstrucción del mundo de los familiares de desaparecidos*. La Plata: Ediciones Al Margen, 2001.
• Derrida, Jacques *Cada vez única. El fin del mundo*. Trans. Manuel Arranz. Valencia: Pre-Textos, 2005.
• Espinosa, Francisco, Julián Casanova, Conxita Mir, Francisco Moreno Gómez. *Morir, matar, sobrevivir: La violencia en la dictadura de Franco*. Barcelona: Booket, 2004.
• Etxeberría Gabilondo, Francisco, Julio Vidal, Santiago Macias, Lourdes Herrasti Erlogorri, F. Pastor, and María Encina. Prada. 'Antropología del pasado reciente: una fosa común de la Guerra Civil Española en Priaranza del Bierzo (León)'. *Antropología y biodiversidad* 1 (2002): pp. 431–446
• Ferrándiz, Francisco. *El pasado bajo tierra*. Barcelona: Anthropos, 2014.
• Guglielmucci, Ana 'Posesiones inalienables: conservación y circulación de objetos de personas desaparecidas en la Argentina y Colombia'. *Cuadernos del Centro de Estudios en Diseño y Comunicación* 131 (2021/2022): pp. 51–63.
• Moreno Andrés, Jorge. *El duelo revelado. La vida social de las fotografías familiares de las víctimas del franquismo*. Madrid: Consejo Superior de Investigaciones Científicas, 2018.
• Palacios González, Daniel 'Memoria, ética y educación desde las fosas comunes: más allá del duelo y el monumento'. In 'Debate: Comunidades de práctica y el futuro de la educación ilemata'. Eds. Marina Garcés and Antonio Casado da Rocha. *Revista Internacional de Éticas Aplicadas*, no. 33 (2020): pp. 135–146.
• Panizo, Laura Mariana. 'Cuerpo, velatorio y performance' *Revista Tán@to's* 13 (2012): pp. 24–35.
• Panizo, Laura Mariana. '"Qué pena me da la pena": duelo, pena y rituales de paso en familiares de desaparecidos de la dictadura de Pinochet (Chile)'. *Disparidades. Revista de Antropología* 79, no. 2, e984 (2024): pp. 2–12.
• Salazar, Andrade, Jose Alonso, Stefanía Acevedo Nossa, Daniela González Ríos, and Laura M. Buitrago Saldarriaga. *Memoria, violencia lineal y pena moral: narrativas de la masacre de Trujillo*. Medellín: Editorial Kavilando, 2019.
• Tzuc, Efraín. 'Contar para no buscar, la paradoja del registro de las desapariciones'. *Adónde Van Los Desaparecidos*. 19 May 2022. https://adondevanlosdesaparecidos.org/2022/05/19/registro-contador-despariciones-mexico/.

Black on White

Jana Traboulsi

262-63, Jana Traboulsi, *The Forms of Leaving and the Forms of Returning*, 2009, drawing of birds carrying back the walls of homes, the family pictures of those who had to flee war, their villages destroyed. Courtesy of Jana Traboulsi

Jana Traboulsi, *We Carry Our Children Every Night, Some of Us for the Last Time*, 2023. Since the start of the genocide in Gaza, images of mothers and fathers carrying the bodies of their children started circulating online. I cannot but notice how sleep and death are alike, when I sing a lullaby for my son to sleep. Courtesy of Jana Traboulsi

Jana Traboulsi, *Free Palestine*, 2023. Inspired by the Palestinian keffiyeh, the illustrator turns the olive leaves into flying birds. Courtesy of Jana Traboulsi

Jana Traboulsi, *Genocide in Instalments*, 2014, drawing of several bombs dropping each with a different date: 'Gaza 2004', 'Gaza 2006', 'Gaza 2008', 'Gaza 2012', 'Gaza 2014'. The artwork is highlighting the repeated aggression of Israel against Gaza. Courtesy of Jana Traboulsi

[redacted]

Something Smiles Through All the Drowsiness of the World

A Field Report

Maha Maamoun

The year 2011 brought to the Arab world what felt like revolution—a sweeping wave of uprisings against the old, stagnant status quo, with its inequitable and exhausted solutions, as well as a surge of new possibilities and questions: from the immediate and pragmatic questions of how to source water and electricity to sustain the thousands of protesters in the squares, to quirkier questions like how to build a catapult to defend a street, or more speculative long-term questions of how to move, think, feel, and live differently.

Reclaiming agency and access to public space—physically, politically, and poetically—was something many of us worked towards in our different practices prior to, during, and after 2011. As artists, curators, and managers/founders of independent arts organizations in our respective cities (Amman and Cairo), Ala Younis and myself shared a concern for expanding access to the sites and languages of art beyond the limited reach of designated art spaces. As artists and cultural producers, we believed in the relevance and need for the perspectives and languages offered by artists, and that these languages are not, or need not be, as exclusive or inaccessible as they are often made to be.

In 2012, we founded Kayfa ta—a publishing initiative that uses the popular format of how-to manuals to respond to some of the perceived needs and desires of the moment, be they the development of skills, tools, thoughts, or sensibilities. We chose the familiar format and methods of how-to books, a popular genre prevalent on streetside bookstands as well as in museum shops, as an entry point: a form through which we can pass other forms. We situated these inexpensive pocket-sized manuals in the space between the technical and the reflective, the everyday and the speculative, the instructional and the intuitive, and the factual and the fictional.

Kayfa ta started by inviting authors, who we believed had a keen sensitivity to the moment we were living through, to propose a question and reflect on it with a general audience. In the loud and hyper-visible moment of Arab revolutions, it was emblematic that the first question published in our series was *How to Disappear*—an exploration of the limits of individuality and collectivity, and how to move fluidly between these modes of perception and action, of self- and group organization, that is at once inward- and outward-looking; a sensibility that would find resonance in subsequent publications.[1] In hindsight, if I were to identify some of the main themes running through these different manuals, it may be the concern with knowledge and its sources and values, be they known or sublimated, personal or institutional, canonized or rejected: identifying areas of pain and loss, of beauty and promise, while forging processes of thought and action that can accompany us through these different questions.[2]

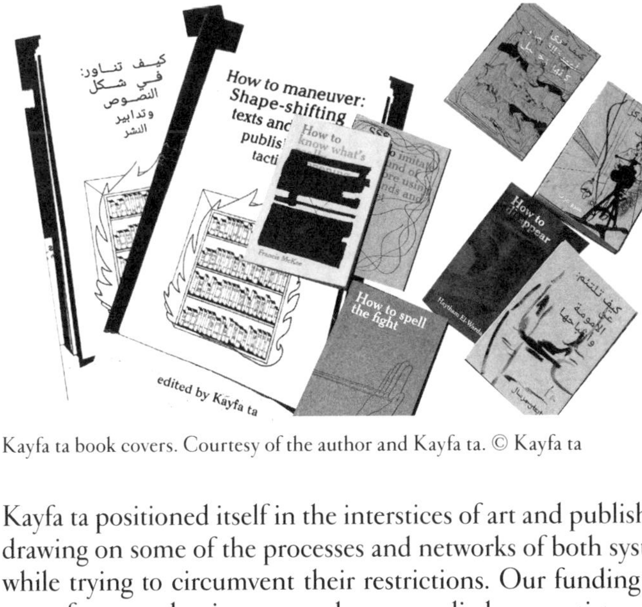

Kayfa ta book covers. Courtesy of the author and Kayfa ta. © Kayfa ta

Kayfa ta positioned itself in the interstices of art and publishing, drawing on some of the processes and networks of both systems while trying to circumvent their restrictions. Our funding first came from production grants that we applied to as artists with a publishing initiative, and increasingly through institutional invitations and the proceeds from sales. We worked, printed, and distributed in different cities without having a base in any, in collaboration with a growing number of individual and institutional partners.

As we moved from one manual to the next, our sense of the publishing contexts we were operating in grew, and with it a

[redacted]

keen curiosity about alternative publishing practices and histories. Who chose to, or had to, publish off the grid? How did they do so, and what were the contexts they were operating in and against? How did they position themselves and their projects, and what local and international networks did they intentionally foster or deliberately disconnect from? These questions, equally relevant to the art contexts in which we work, instigated ongoing research into the precarious, significant, and largely invisible practices of independent publishing in our region. These practices played an important role in challenging the restrictive publishing regimes of their time, yet remain little-known, their publications hard to find, and their histories scantily written.

We Could Not Remember Any Precedents

> ***It was not an easy matter. Producing a magazine outside the framework of the official institutions was a dangerous venture, both for the magazine itself and for those who produce it. Moreover, we could not remember any precedents that would serve to illuminate our way, as not one cultural magazine had been produced outside of state supervision since 1952 [...].***[3]
> —Ibrahim Mansour

Ibrahim Mansour was one of the founders of the cultural magazine *Gallery 68* (1968–1971). It was founded in the aftermath of the 1967 Arab-Israeli war, with its overwhelming sense of national defeat. A sense of betrayal by leadership, with its monolithic policies and rhetoric, instigated processes of individual and collective soul-searching and critical revisions. This gave birth to a need to reappropriate publishing from the hegemony of the state. *Gallery 68* was thus founded and supported by some of the most prominent writers and artists of the day. Mansour explains that 'intellectuals of the day had to strive not only to develop alternative cultural values but also to create new modes of communication that affirm the right to express, create and publish. They had to found their own independent magazines [...].'[4] After publishing eight issues, their licence was finally revoked by the Egyptian Ministry of Culture.[5]

Twenty years later, in 1991, poet Hisham Keshta was impelled to start *al-Kitaba al-'Ukhra* (*The Other Writing*), one of the longer-lived independent periodicals from that period. Keshta recalls two main incidents that sparked this new publication. First, a fight with the renowned editor of one of the state-owned magazines, who had stated, on assumption of his editorial duties, that the magazine is for the 'elite' and not the 'riff-raff' (of writers). The second incident, which is more foundational for Keshta, is the reappearance of Anwar Kamel, a member of the Egyptian surrealist Art and Liberty group and founder of the group's radical magazine *al-Tatawur* (January–September 1940).[6] Little is known of Kamel's life and practice for the forty or so years after the closure of the magazine, until he reappeared in a café in downtown Cairo in the late 1980s, where he actively sought out the younger generation of writers and started hand-distributing his new *al-Fasa'il* publication, collaborating with Hisham Keshta on the founding of *al-Kitaba al-'Ukhra*.

> *Anwar Kamel announced then that he smells the scent of the Art and Liberty group in the texts of this new generation. And so, he started his new publication,* al-Fasa'il *[...] which was a mixture of texts by the Art and Liberty group with new texts, thus affirming the spiritual affinity of the two generations. A hundred copies, which Kamel wrote on his typewriter [then photocopied] and brought to us every Tuesday at [Zahret] al-Bustan café, handing them to us with his famous saying, 'This is your gift.' We were looking for inspiring precursors instead of the hideous mutants that the authorities imposed on us; we were looking for a lineage of our choice. When I saw Kamel, I remembered George Henein's verse: 'On some table, something smiles through all the drowsiness of the world.' [...] When I first turned the pages of* al-Tatawur *magazine, I said to myself: this is a language we can build on, and these are thoughts we can engage with, this magazine alone can be considered a cultural root for us.*[7]

In another encounter in a café in Tangiers, Moroccan writer Mohamed Choukri exclaimed upon seeing the acclaimed writer Mohamed Al-Sabbagh in Tangier's Continental Café: 'I had no

[redacted]

idea that writers might actually be seen in public places [...] writers were either very private people or they were dead.'[8] This remark triggered Haytham El-Wardany's reflection on the elusive location of the writer, within and beyond their present time and place, and on the meaning of invisibility and death here.

The most natural place for one engaged in writing might not be the given present but rather the point at which the present opens up to its future or past. Meaning, the point at which it becomes possible to transcend the present through an attempt to summon that which has been removed from it.[9]

This fascinating essay that tries to read into the ontology of writing and the role of the writer, ideally, comes very close to describing the place and impetus for independent publishing which one feels in the more remarkable projects. When Anwar Kamel met Hisham Keshta and his generation of writers, they reminded each other of that which had been excluded from their realities: the kind of writing and publishing that they once had or wished to have. Their meeting inspired a cultural magazine that was rich, confrontational, and relatively long-lived—it ran for ten years, paused for ten years, then returned for one issue in 2011 to celebrate the Egyptian revolution. Their meeting also inspired the reprinting of *al-Tatawur* magazine, decades after its closure and the disappearance of any trace of it. For on his deathbed, Kamel beseeched Keshta to republish *al-Tatawur*, a photocopy of which he had managed to get to Keshta from a friend in Paris. Bound by his promise to Kamel, Keshta sought for means to realize Kamel's dying wish, and eventually accepted an offer, made by Samir Gharib, who was then head of the governmental Fund for Cultural Development, to reprint both *al-Tatawur* and *Gallery 68*, accepting this collaboration with a governmental body as long as it was limited to the republication of cultural heritage, without them meddling in the contemporary cultural scene. The remaining idle copies and scans of *al-Kitaba al-'Ukhra*'s edition of these cultural magazines remain a rare and valuable resource, contributing greatly to bringing these publishing histories back to light and tracing some of the literary, cultural, and political lineages and persuasions that ran through these alternative cultural projects.

How to Reappear

When we received, as a curatorial duo, an invitation in 2019 from Beirut Art Center (BAC) to curate an exhibition for their space, we steered this invitation towards Kayfa ta and its growing interest in the field of independent publishing. We proposed 'How to Reappear: Through the Quivering Leaves of Independent Publishing', an exhibition and public programme of existing and newly commissioned publications, research projects, and artworks that reflect on contemporary practices and histories of publishing, with a strong focus on Arab and resonant international practices.

The exhibition opened at BAC in September 2019 and was invited soon after by Warehouse421 (Abu Dhabi), opening in December 2019, and by MMAG (Amman), opening in January 2020.[10] The exhibition's form and constellation of projects changed from one city to the next, in conversation with the local publishing histories and practices. Works presented were not limited to publications, but also included works that engaged through media such as sculpture and performance with some of the key concerns of publishing. Some works gave an overview of specific histories of publishing, like Bernhard Cella's sculptural and research works that explore the domain of publications printed without an ISBN. Cella had made his first call for submissions of such books in 2009, through flyers that he posted outside of the NY Art Book Fair. With the books received, he produced several installations, as well as an online platform and book register. The register, which included a total of 1,800 recent no-ISBN print publications, investigates extraordinary books that withdraw, deliberately or accidentally, from the visibility of international book trade conduits. In preparation for 'How to Reappear', we invited Cella to renew his call, ten years after his first, this time for publications from Arabic-speaking countries. The books received were then organized and presented as a sculpture, which users were able to peruse, of that shadow ecology of books produced in our region. A selection of these was presented in the Arabic edition of Cella's book *NO-ISBN: On Self-Publishing*, which Kayfa ta translated and published in

[redacted]

collaboration with Warehouse421 in the context of the exhibition there.[11]

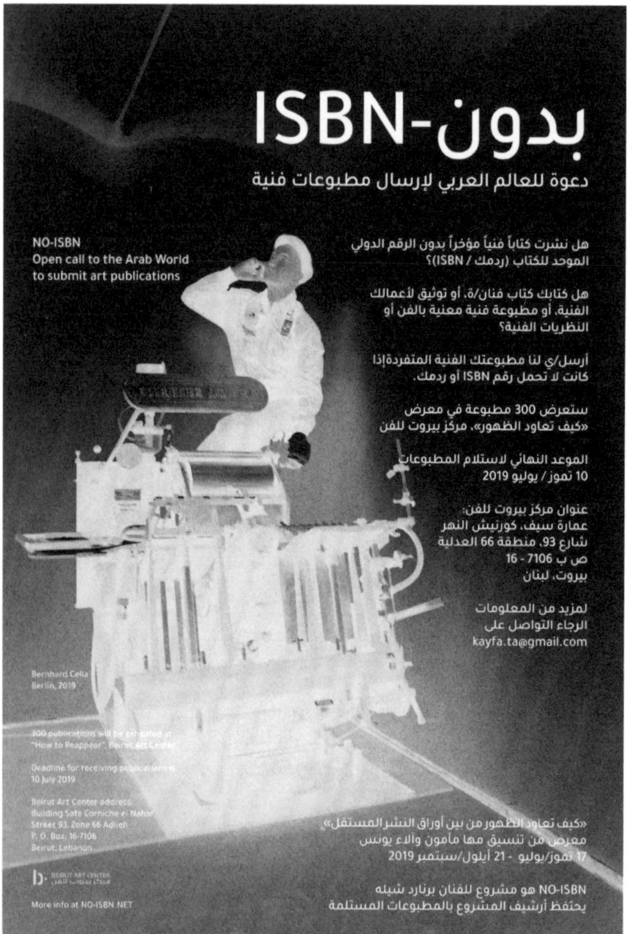

The open call for the Arabic edition of Bernhard Cella's 'NO-ISBN' project presented in 'How to Reappear: Through the Quivering Leaves of Independent Publishing', Beirut Art Center (BAC), 2019. Courtesy of the author and Kayfa ta. © Kayfa ta

Kayfa ta, 'How to Reappear: Through the Quivering Leaves of Independent Publishing', Beirut Art Center (BAC), 2019, as part of Bernhard Cella's 'NO-ISBN: On Self-Publishing' (Arabic edition) project. Courtesy of the author and Kayfa ta. © Kayfa ta

Another installation was of Simone Fattal's Post-Apollo Press, which she founded in 1982 in Sausalito, California, after fleeing there from the Lebanese Civil War. Specializing in poetry, experimental writing, and translation, the Post-Apollo Press became an important player in the Bay Area publishing scene. Fattal stopped her art practice for an extended period of immersion in the minutiae of directing and sustaining an independent publishing house, from one book to the next. She resumed her art practice many years later, but remained for a long time mainly known in the United States as a publisher and in the Arab world as an artist. We presented in Beirut for the first time the almost full set of Post-Apollo publications, as well as a large selection of unpublished working documents from the Post-Apollo Press, gathered from the artist's own archive and from the Bancroft Library at the University of California, Berkeley. This presentation on a twelve-metre table gave a rare insight into the history of this important publishing project: the invisible backstage work of editing drafts, cover designs, book dummies, and colour corrections, and the letters to and from printers, distributors,

[redacted]

authors, and readers. It presented the full feel of what it means to conceive and carry through a serious independent publishing project.

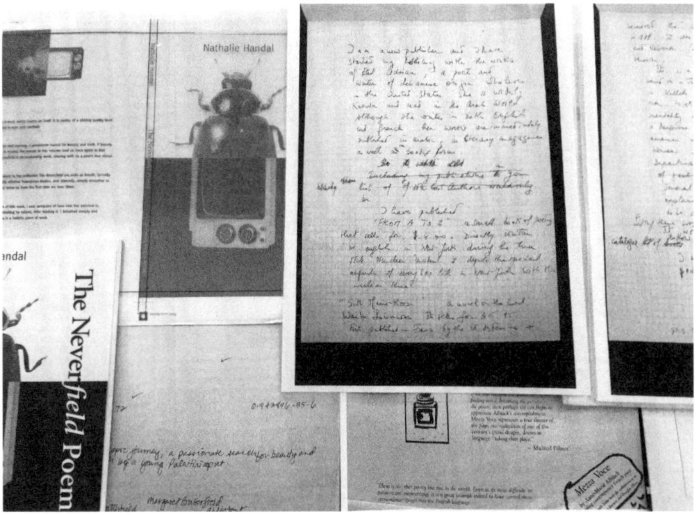

Detail of the installation of the work of The Post-Apollo Press at 'How to Re-appear: Through the Quivering Leaves of Independent Publishing', Beirut Art Center (BAC), 2019. Courtesy of the author and Kayfa ta. © Kayfa ta

Other works focused more on specific aspects of publishing—questions of form, circulation, visibility, public-making, distribution, legibility, resistance, and many others. We concluded this three-part exhibition cycle with a reader that brought together a selection of the artworks, research, and writing that informed or was presented through the exhibitions. It would be difficult to give an idea of how diverse and special these projects were in the space of this text. But maybe a look through the contents of the *How to Maneuver* reader can give an overall idea of some of the threads running through the exhibitions and research.

And Now?

About two years into the televised genocide, deliberate starvation, and obliteration of what remains of Gaza and its people, now feels less of a moment of possibility than the one experienced at the beginning of the Arab revolutions. On the best of days, it is a moment of proceeding 'with-neither-hope-nor-despair', as described years after by Amr Ezzat in *How to Remember*

Your Dreams, or rather of proceeding *with*-hope-and-despair against the background of an ongoing genocide, glaring political inefficacy and complicity, and the promise of a growing resistance movement coming from the sidelines. How many manoeuvres and how much shapeshifting would be needed to survive and push through the presiding political system? Will we be able to see through the heart of this present moment, and in so doing summon, from a past or future, 'that which has been removed from it'? And what can 'that' be? In the meantime, we will ask ourselves anew questions that we had asked in the beginning: Who will choose to, or will be forced to, publish off the grid? How will they do so, and what are the challenges they are operating in and against? How will they position themselves and their projects, and what local and international networks will they wilfully foster or deliberately disconnect from?

CONTENTS

5 FOREWORD
Faisal Al Hassan

8 INTRODUCTION
Maha Maamoun and Ala Younis

THE POSSIBILITY OF TRANSCENDING REALITY

13 THE PLACE OF THE WRITER
OR, THE IMPORTANCE OF WRITERS BEING DEAD
Haytham el-Wardany

19 PAPER NOR ME_XX2:
BEYOND THE PAPER PRINCIPLE
Moad Musbahi

29 A TRILOGY: PALM TREES LEAVE THEIR PLACE, TEXTS CHANGE THEIR FORM
Hussein Nassereddine

40 BOOKWORM
Farah Khelil & antoine lefebvre editions

45 A SHORT HISTORY OF THE STATE
The State

57 EARTH BUILDING
Ahmad Makia

MANEUVERING HISTORY

69 THE MAKING OF PRINTED IN BEIRUT
Jabbour Douaihy

73 HISTORY OF THE BOOK IN LEBANON
Hala Bizri

79 VISUAL MODERNITY IN INDIA: LITTLE MAGAZINES AND THE VERNACULAR PUBLIC SPHERE
Noopur Desai

93 THROUGH THE WORLD WILD WEB
Jaffat El Aqlam

103 BORROWED FACES: STORIES OF PUBLISHERS DURING THE COLD WAR
Fehras Publishing Practices

131 PUBLISHING AS AGENT OF CULTURAL ENGAGEMENT: BEIRUT (mid 1940s–early 1980s)
Huda Smitshuijzen AbiFarès

157 MASTER REVOLUTION
THE STORY OF A DEMOCRACY ON PAPER
Ali Hussein Al-Adawy

181 A DIALOG BETWEEN RHYTHM AND FORM
Khalid Albudoor and Nujoom Alghanem in conversation with Rand Abdul Jabbar, Uns Kattan and Hammad Nasar

226 SCRAPBOOK
Bady Dalloul

SHAPESHIFTING TEXTS AND OTHER PUBLISHING TACTICS

235 THE RAINY DAYS SERIES
Ali Yass

243 REBELS THE WORLD OVER—SAY BARA
Barakunan

249 SALON SALON
Bernhard Cella

255 GETTING LIGHTER, STILL LABOUR-INTENSIVE
Elaine W. HO

269 THE PROPOSAL AS A PUBLICATION FORMAT
Raafat Majzoub

279 PUBLISHING AT POINT ZERO
Yazan Ashqar

287 GHOSTED PUBLICS—THE 'UNACKNOWLEDGED COLLECTIVE' IN THE CONTEMPORARY TRANSFORMATION OF THE CIRCULATION OF IDEAS
Andrew Murphie

297 UNLEARNING HOW TO
TACTICS FOR DAILY POETICS:
A CONVERSATION WITH KAYFA TA
Federico Antonini & Giulia Crispiani

312 NO PART OF THIS BOOK MAY BE REPRODUCED, IN ANY WAY, BY PHOTOCOPYING, RECORDING, OR OTHERWISE, EXCEPT WITH THE PRIOR WRITTEN CONSENT OF THE PUBLISHER
Ali Eyal

321 BIOGRAPHIES 329 PARTICIPANTS 334 IMPRINT

Table of contents of *How to Maneuver: Shapeshifting Texts and Other Publishing Tactics*, 2019. Courtesy of the author and Kayfa ta. © Kayfa ta

Notes

1 • Haytham El-Wardany, *How to Disappear* (Amman: Kayfa ta, 2013).
2 • Questions proposed later include *How to Imitate the Sound of the Shore Using Two Hands and a Carpet* by Cevdet Erek (2014); *How to Know What's Really Happening* by Francis McKee (2016); *How to Mend: Motherhood and Its Ghosts* by Iman Mersal (2017); *How to Spell the Fight* by Natascha Haghighian (2018); *How to Remember Your Dreams* by Amr Ezzat (2019); *How to See Palace Pillars As If They Were Palm Trees* by Hussein Nassereddine (2019); *How to Love a Homeland* by Oxana Timofeeva (2021); and *How to Make Female Action Heroes* by Madhusree Dutta (2023).
3 • Ibrahim Mansour, 'Gallery 68', *al-Kitaba al-'Ukhra*, no. 7 (February 1994), p. 8.
4 • Amgad Rayyan, 'On the Experience of Ida'a 77', *al-Kitaba al-'Ukhra*, no. 7 (February 1994), p. 13.
5 • An ephemeral wave of independent publishing then ensued, arising from across Egypt, using a cheap printing technique and a legal loophole to print and circulate a variety of literary and artistic publications. The Master movement lasted from the 1970s until the 1990s. It took its name from its cheap printing technique that creates a 'master' paper print that is then used for reproduction. Mostly used for printing cheap paper advertisements, this technology was appropriated by writers to inexpensively produce non-periodic cultural magazines across Egypt. Kayfa ta commissioned writer and researcher Ali Hussein Al-Adawy to conduct a series of interviews with some of the key players in the Master scene of the 1970s–1990s, commencing ongoing research on the Master movement and its context, strategies, and influences in the history of alternative publishing in Egypt. Ali Hussein Al-Adawy, 'The Master Movement: A Democracy on Paper', in *How to Maneuver: Shapeshifting Texts and Other Publishing Tactics*, eds. Maha Maamoun and Ala Younis (Abu Dhabi: Kayfa ta and Warehouse421, 2019), pp. 157–180.
6 • In January 1940, the first issue of *al-Tatawur* magazine came out, published by the Egyptian surrealist Arts and Liberty group and funded by Anwar Kamel, one of the group's prominent figures. Though the magazine did not announce a political affiliation, its radical, iconoclastic voice leaned clearly to the left, calling for a minimum wage and fixed working hours, as well as artistic and moral liberation from the shackles of convention. The magazine lasted for seven issues, until it finally had to close under pressure from the British Embassy, the Palace, and Al-Azhar.
7 • Hisham Keshta, 'But They Made the Future: In Loving Memory of Anwar Kamel on the 25th Anniversary of His Departure', in *Al-Tatawur: The Magazine of the Art and Liberty Group. The Complete Issues* (January–September 1940), ed. Hisham Keshta (Cairo: Dar Elias for printing and publishing, 2016), pp. 9–13.

[redacted]

8 • Haytham el-Wardany, 'The Place of the Writer, or The Importance of Writers Being Dead', in Maamoun and Younis, *How to Maneuver*, p. 13.
9 • Ibid., p. 17.
10 • News of a pandemic was gradually reaching us. Airports would lock down worldwide a few months later, in April 2020.
11 • Bernhard Cella et al., *NO-ISBN: On Self-Publishing* (New York: Printed Matter, 2015), and Bernhard Cella et al., *NO-ISBN: On Self-Publishing*, Arabic edition (Beirut and Vienna: Kayfa ta and Salon für Kunstbuch, 2023).
12 • Maamoun and Younis, *How to Maneuver.*
13 • Amr Ezzat, *How to Remember Your Dreams* (Beirut: Kayfa ta, 2021).

[redacted]

Hold on to Her
On Grief and Ritual Justice

Pascal Gielen

Who remembers Mawda? Perhaps today she would be giving her first school presentation—shy, but proud. Perhaps she once dreamed of becoming a doctor, a dancer, a lawyer. Perhaps, in some other future, she would now be cycling through British streets with an untroubled smile. But it was not to be.

On 17 May 2018, two-year-old Mawda Shawri—a Kurdish-Iraqi toddler—was shot dead by a Belgian police officer on a highway near Mons. She was in a van fleeing with her parents, younger brother, and other migrants towards the United Kingdom. A shot was fired during the chase. It proved fatal.

What followed made the tragedy even more painful. Mawda's parents were arrested and denied the chance to hold their daughter one last time. Amnesty International and the Human Rights League criticized the lack of transparency. Initially, it was denied that a police bullet had killed her; only months later did the full truth emerge. To this day, the Belgian state continues to repress the story.

The media too played a role in covering up the painful reality. Rather than focus on a trigger-happy police officer and failing migration policy, the narrative quickly shifted to 'people smuggling' and 'illegal migration'—as if Mawda's death were the fault of her parents. The distortion was noticed far beyond Belgium. Philosopher Noam Chomsky pointed to the bizarre inversion: when laws criminalize the victims, justice is turned upside down.

The Non-Place of Justice

Mawda was not killed in a warzone. No bombs fell that night. And yet her death belongs to a necropolitical landscape shaped by another kind of violence: the violence of migration policy, of EU border regimes, of laws that kill without aiming, and aim without guilt.

This logic is nowhere more clearly embodied than in the operations of Frontex, the European Border and Coast Guard Agency. Although not yet active in Belgium at the time of Mawda's death, Frontex has since become a key player in enforcing Europe's hardened border regimes—not just at the external edges of the continent, but increasingly within member states' own territories. Officially tasked with 'border security', the agency now patrols not only physical borders, but legal thresholds as well, slipping between national jurisdictions and EU accountability. Its actions are often shrouded in opacity, subcontracted to private firms, and answerable to no democratic public in particular. With recent legislation allowing Frontex to operate on Belgian soil, even domestic territory is transformed into a kind of frontier. As if the border were no longer a line, but a diffuse condition. A mood.

And in this mood, the law itself begins to deform. As Giorgio Agamben notes in *Homo Sacer*, the sovereign power lies in the ability to declare a 'state of exception'—a moment where law is suspended to supposedly protect it. But what happens when the exception becomes the norm? When it no longer appears as crisis but as administration?

Refugees, in Agamben's terms, become bare life—stripped of political value, legally present but not protected. Outside the law's guarantees, yet still subject to its force. They are no longer rights-bearing individuals but *homo sacer*: sacred in the ancient Roman sense, meaning they may be killed but not mourned. Executable, but not sacrificial. And once labelled 'illegal', even a child becomes eligible for disappearance.

We saw how this logic operates in the United States. Under the pretext of foreign policy authority, President Donald Trump blocked the return of Kilmar Ábrego García, who was deported without hesitation despite a judicial ban on expulsion. The label 'illegal' sufficed to deactivate legal protection—even against the ruling of the Supreme Court.

Europe externalizes such states of exception, pushing them beyond its borders to camps in Libya or through deals with Turkey. The rule of law seems unable to confront its own moral failure, and so it displaces it. But when this very same logic returns to domestic soil, as in the case of Mawda's death, the response is denial, evasion, and silence. Not by accident, but as a symptom—a symptom of a political order in which legal principles are sacrificed to a politics of exclusion.

[redacted]

Rituals Undone

There was a public funeral for Mawda, but no national commemoration. No prime minister's speech. There was a trial—eventually. A courtroom with sharp suits and blurred memories, but the state that ended her life did not ritually account for it.

And yet such rituals matter. As Byung-Chul Han argues in *The Disappearance of Rituals*, a society without symbolic forms of recognition becomes a desert of meaning. Without shared gestures—of mourning, of remembrance, of responsibility—a society cannot reproduce its own ethical foundations. It forgets how to feel together. And then, slowly, it forgets what it is.

Justice is not just a matter of rules. It requires rhythm. The solemn pace of a trial, the choreography of a public apology, the echo of names spoken aloud in commemoration. These are not aesthetic niceties. They are the soul of the rule of law. Without them, law becomes nothing but management. Without them, Mawda's death becomes an administrative error, a 'tragic incident', a regrettable inconvenience. Collateral damage. The absence of ritual is not neutral. It is a deliberate act of refusing to remember.

Robin Vanbesien remembered. In his film *hold on to her*, made in close collaboration with the post-collective—an open, multi-voiced platform of artists, activists, and researchers—he refused the silence. No forensic reconstruction, no dramatic reenactments. Instead, he created a space—half poetic, half documentary—where voices of witnesses, friends, and family braided together around Mawda's absence. There is singing. There is archival footage. There is time. Time to feel. Time to reflect.

Vanbesien, trained as a visual artist and philosopher, works at the intersections of political thought, documentary, and art. His oeuvre often explores the hidden infrastructures of state violence and collective memory. Rather than explaining or illustrating, he crafts aesthetic forms of listening, sensing, and mourning that unsettle the rational scaffolding of public discourse.

Vanbesien is not a journalist. He is an artist of fragility. His work does not shout. It hums. It listens. It dares to mourn publicly, in a Europe that increasingly treats mourning as a weakness and bureaucratic silence as strength. The film is a ritual—not to sanctify the state, but to rehumanize its victims.

Here, grief becomes political again. Not as spectacle, but as what Judith Butler calls 'a mode of political responsiveness'. To grieve Mawda is to contest her erasure. To grieve is to refuse the abstraction that turned her body into collateral. In this sense, *hold on to her* performs a rare thing: a justice that moves beyond jurisprudence. It remembers a girl not just with facts, but with form—with rhythm, breath, voice. In the absence of bombs, this film offers resonance.

Grief as Refusal

Grief, it is often said, is a private matter. A solitary passage through pain, memory, and disorientation. In this view—one widely held in the psychotherapeutic tradition—grief belongs to the individual psyche, to the bedroom, to the internal dialogues no state can regulate and no court can fully hear. As Julia Samuel reminds us in *Grief Works*, grieving is a necessary and intimate response to rupture, but it remains ethically and politically incomplete if it cannot be transformed into mourning.

It is precisely this transformation—from the inwardness of grief to the outwardness of mourning—that marks the boundary between private loss and collective responsibility. As Guy Cools argues in *Performing Mourning*, the act of mourning is never merely emotional; it is a performative gesture, embedded in time, space, and social structure. Mourning, unlike grief, requires a witness. It asks for an audience—not to console the bereaved, but to co-carry the meaning of what was lost, and to name the forces that made such loss possible.

This distinction is not merely semantic. It is political. For in the refusal to allow grief to mature into mourning—in the decision to treat sorrow as a personal defect rather than a collective wound—the state reveals its deeper unwillingness to be held accountable. A system that bureaucratically acknowledges a death without ritually recognizing it, performs not only an administrative evasion, but an ontological one. It severs the bond between law and meaning, between justice and symbolic reparation. The legal system, when stripped of its capacity to mourn, becomes a machine of forgetting.

Such a polity that suppresses mourning forfeits one of the key instruments of democratic regeneration. For mourning—in its shared, performative, and ritual forms—is not only a cultural response to death, but a mechanism for the relegitimation of power. It is the space where states can admit their failures without collapsing, where law can regain its face not through punishment but through vulnerability.

Without mourning, grief calcifies. The private becomes pathological. Citizens are asked to metabolize unbearable losses on their own, often with the implicit message that to grieve publicly is to disrupt the social order. Yet precisely this disruption is what makes mourning politically potent. It interrupts the flow of denial. It slows down the machinery of forgetting. It calls for the presence of others—not merely as spectators, but as co-mourners, as co-responsible agents in the unfinished project of justice.

To block this process is not a neutral act. It is a strategy—a deliberate containment of affect in order to protect the symbolic economy of the state. It is no coincidence that authoritarian and technocratic regimes are often allergic to public mourning. For to mourn together is to make space for dissent, for reflection, for the unsettling truth that not all suffering is accidental.

In this sense, mourning is not the end of politics, but its re-entry point. It is where a society rehearses a different kind of sovereignty—one grounded not in force or control, but in recognition, humility, and symbolic accountability. And perhaps this is the most radical gesture mourning can offer: the suggestion that justice is not merely a matter of procedures and verdicts, but of how a society chooses to remember, and whom it allows to be remembered.

A state that cannot mourn is a state that cannot be trusted. And a legal system that refuses ritual grief will, eventually, become law without justice—a corpse with no breath of legitimacy. Such a body politic has lost all authority and can do nothing but hold on to power. When legitimacy disappears, power must be enforced. Authority becomes brute command, and law becomes indistinguishable from order. In such a regime, sovereignty depends no longer on recognition but on repression. It no longer governs with consent, but with coercion. And when even fear fails, it resorts to the final measure—to survive, it needs a bloody war.

References

- Agamben, Giorgio. *Homo Sacer: Sovereign Power and Bare Life.* Trans. Daniel Heller-Roazen. Stanford University Press, 1998.
- Arendt, Hannah. *Eichmann in Jerusalem: A Report on the Banality of Evil.* New York: Viking Press, 1963.
- Butler, Judith. *Precarious Life: The Powers of Mourning and Violence.* New York: Verso, 2004.
- Cools, Guy. *Performing Mourning: Laments in Contemporary Art.* Amsterdam: Valiz, 2021.
- Chomsky, Noam. Public lectures and interventions on asylum, justice, and the erosion of legal norms, 2020.
- Gielen, Pascal. *Trust: Building on the Cultural Commons.* Amsterdam: Valiz, 2024.
- Han, Byung-Chul. *The Disappearance of Rituals: A Topology of the Present.* Trans. Daniel Steuer. Cambridge, UK: Polity Press, 2020.
- Samuel, Julia. *Grief Works: Stories of Life, Death and Surviving.* New York: Penguin Random House, 2017.
- Vanbesien, Robin. *hold on to her.* Film. 2022.

[redacted]

Drawings
Walid Taher

Walid Taher's works reflect the pre-revolution sentiment, while the last drawing captures the sentiment of the actual revolution. Including him as a link between an older generation of designers in this volume like Mohammed Hijji and younger ones like Jana Traboulsi reflects a lineage of Arab artists and designers who channelled the concerns of the people.

pp. 20–21	*You Sons of Bitches*, 2005
pp. 34–35	*Flammable Material*, 2011
pp. 128–129	*Human Rights*, 2009
pp. 222–223	*They Humiliated, Belittled, Impoverished, Silenced Me and Made Me Disbelieve in the Divine, They Categorized, Hurt and Blew Me Up. I Exploded, I Won, I Was Happy, I Flew, Now It's Your Turn to Join Me*, 2011

[redacted]

Contributors

Contributors

Abdul Wahhab Al-Bayati (1926–1999) was an Iraqi poet and writer. He is considered one of four contributors to the founding of the new school of Arabic poetry in Iraq (the pioneers of free verse), along with Nazik Al-Malaika, Badr Shakir al-Sayyab, and Shadhil Taqa.

Diana Al-Halabi (1990) is a Rotterdam-Beirut-based interdisciplinary artist working primarily with film and painting. Through an intersectional feminist lens, her practice navigates the entanglement of the personal and the political, challenging top-down structures of power—from the patriarchal gaze and institutional violence to bureaucracy, settler colonialism, migration, visa regimes, and the politicization of the digestive system.

Al-Halabi holds an MFA from the Piet Zwart Institute (2021) in Rotterdam and completed a fellowship at Ashkal Alwan's Home Workspace Program (2018) in Beirut. Her work has been exhibited and screened at IFFR (Rotterdam), Raindance (UK), Black Star Film Festival (USA), Darb 1718 (Cairo), MAO Museum (Torino), Radius CCA (Delft), Garage (Rotterdam), Kiosk (Ghent), Sursock Museum (Beirut), and more.
www.dianahalabi.com

Muzaffar al-Nawwab (1934–2022) was an Iraqi poet and political critic. Dubbed the 'poet of the smuggled poem', he was persecuted and imprisoned in Iraq and subsequently lived in several capitals, including Beirut, Damascus, and other European cities. He is often described as one of the most famous Iraqi poets of the modern era.

Samih al-Qasim (1939–2014) was a Palestinian poet whose name is associated with the poetry of revolution and resistance. He was an active member in the Communist Party before leaving the party to devote himself to his literary work.

Badr Shakir al-Sayyab (1926–1964) was an Iraqi poet, regarded as one of the most important contemporary Arab poets. Alongside Nazik Al-Malaika, he is considered one of the founders of Arab free-verse poetry.

Amir Ashkar is a Palestinian philosopher, winemaker, and activist whose work explores time, trauma, and identity. He is currently pursuing a PhD on the relationship between Being and festivals in Nietzsche's thought. Amir is from the displaced community of Iqrit and the co-founder of Return, an initiative that reclaims original homes without waiting for the occupier's approval.

Tammam Azzam was born in Damascus, lives and works in Berlin, and is represented by Kornfeld Gallery. He graduated from the Faculty of Fine Arts, Department of Painting, in Damascus, in 2001. His works have been shown in exhibitions in the Middle East, Europe and the US, e.g. at Ayyam Gallery in Dubai, at Art Dubai and Untitled Miami as well as at Haines Gallery San Francisco. His works can be found in renowned institutions such as the Barjeel Art Foundation in Sharjah, the Atassi Foundation or the For Site Foundation in San Francisco.
www.tammamazzam.com

Jan Beddegenoodts (1988) is a filmmaker with a gonzo documentary style, and a multidisciplinary artist organizing happenings that address urgent matters. He is the mayor of Cameltown where he gathers his projects. Recent films include: *Searching for Ludo* (2025), *Gamlet* (2024); *Looking for Empathy* (2024); *Groeten uit de Koekenstad* (2022); *Sama' Abdulhadi* (2019); *Thank God It's Friday* (2013); *The Taste of Freedom* (2012). Recent projects include: co-curation of art festival MEERMEER (2025, 2024); 'About Space' (2022); 'Rave & Resist' (festival and happening, Berlin, 2018).
www.cameltown.be

Yousra Benfquih holds a PhD (UAntwerp) in human rights law, for which she was rewarded the Max van der Stoel Human Rights Award. She is also a writer, poet and spoken word artist. Her work has been published in literary magazines such as *Kluger Hans*, *DW B*, *De Poëziekrant*, *De Revisor*, *Etcetera* and

De Gids, while her columns have been featured in journals like *De Standaard*, *Knack* and *De Morgen*. In 2019, she was nominated for the Joost Zwagerman Essay prize. Yousra is an in-house writer for cultural-critical magazine *Rekto:Verso* and teaches Spoken Word at LUCA School of Arts.
www.yousrabenfquih.com

Mahmoud Darwish (1941–2008) was a Palestinian poet and author who was regarded as Palestine's national poet. In 1988 Darwish wrote the Palestinian Declaration of Independence, which was the formal declaration for the creation of a State of Palestine. Darwish won numerous awards for his works.

Julie David de Lossy (1984) is a multimedia specialist and audiovisual producer in the humanitarian sector. She studied Political Sciences at ULB and Conflict, Security and Development at King's College London. Previously a freelance photojournalist, she has worked on visual storytelling across diverse contexts. Since 2022, she leads the Multimedia Team for Médecins Sans Frontières operations in Brussels, developing impactful visual storytelling and communication strategies in humanitarian contexts.

Bruno De Cock (1968) studied photography at the School of Arts in Ghent, Belgium and is currently working with the International Office of Médecins Sans Frontières (MSF) as Audiovisual Senior Advisor. Prior to this he has worked as photography assistant in fashion and advertising photography before moving to the world of news as a photo editor for a local paper. With over 20 years of experience in visual storytelling and content strategy, he is a seasoned professional dedicated to ethical imagery and impactful multimedia narratives in the humanitarian sector. Recently he worked as a Project Manager for the following publications: Juliette Garms, Re-Adjusting the Focus (2024), and Juliette Garms, MSF Audiovisual Storytelling Guidelines (2025).

Jolente De Keersmaeker (1967) is a founding member of TG

STAN. In recent years she created and performed in, among others, *Eind Goed al Goed*, *Bedrog/Trahisons*, *Nora*, *The Cherry Orchard*, *wat/nu*, *Poquelin II*, *Infidèles* and *Revolutionary Road*. Jolente is also regularly involved in the work of her sister, choreographer Anne Teresa De Keersmaeker and her dance company Rosas, and has created two productions with Compagnie Jérôme Bel. Jolente also teaches at the KASK in Ghent and regularly leads workshops in Belgium and abroad. To date, Jolente is artistic director of STAN.

Marlies De Munck (1979) is a philosopher of culture. She is principal research fellow at the Philosophy Department of the University of Antwerp and teaches aesthetics, philosophy of art, and philosophy of music. She supervises artistic research at the Antwerp Research Institute for the Arts. Her writings explore the intersection of art, culture and politics, with a special focus on music. Recent publications include *Why Chopin Did Not Want To Hear The Rain* (2023); *Fragility: To Touch And Be Touched* (with Pascal Gielen) (2022); *I See Mountains Once Again As Mountains* (2021). De Munck lives and works in Antwerp, Belgium.

Damiaan De Schrijver (1962) is a founding member of TG STAN. In recent years he created and performed in, among others, *of/niet*, *Brandhout*, *een irritatie*, *Eg er vinden*, *ik ben de wind*, *wat/nu* and *Poquelin II* and he created performances in collaboration with the members of De Koe, Dood Paard and Maatschappij Discordia, such as *De Beroemden*, *De Toverberg*, *Onomatopée*, *My Dinner with André*, *atelier* and *Warm*. He regularly works on films and TV series, including *Het Verdriet van België* (1995), *Terug naar Oosterdonck* (1997), *Kijk eens op de doos* (2002), *Dennis van Rita* (2006), *De Ronde* (2011), *Met Man en Macht* (2012), *Rosie & Moussa* (2018) and *F**k You Very Much* (2022). To date, Damiaan is artistic director at STAN.

Naama Shoshana Fogiel Lewin (1996) is a performance artist holding an MA in choreography and performance art from ISAC (Arba-Esa). Her practice emerges from dance and movement

[redacted]

and extends into voice, text, and installation. Through her work, she navigates the politics of body, space, land, and identity, developing deconstructive practices that challenge mechanisms of nationalism and militarism. Her performance and installation *To Break Up with I'* has been shown at Amsterdam Fringe Festival (2025), Outside In Festival (Mechelen, 2025), Théâtre de la Vie (Brussels, 2025), Nomad Dance Advocacy (Zagreb, 2024). She was published in *Arts of the Working Class* 37. Her performance *SickHomeLand* is shown in Théâtre de la Vie (Brussels, 2025). Fogiel Lewin lives and works in Brussels.
www.nashfole.kesug.com

Lara García Diaz (1986) is a researcher and educator specializing in social design and the intersection of art-based and design-based research, approached from post-humanist, feminist, and ecological perspectives. She holds a PhD in Social Sciences from the University of Antwerp and the Antwerp Research Institute for the Arts (Belgium). She is lecturer-researcher and coordinator of EINA Research at EINA University of Art and Design, affiliated with the Autonomous University of Barcelona, and leads the Social Design track in the Master's in Applied Research in Design at ELISAVA. She is principal investigator of *Situated Creative Practices for the Pluriverse* (Creative Europe) and researcher in *Responses of Artistic Research to Historical Crisis* (Spanish Ministry of Science and Innovation). She has published in academic and non-academic journals and books and participates in international conferences. García Diaz lives and works in Barcelona.

Pascal Gielen (1970) is writer and full professor of sociology of culture and politics at the Antwerp Research Institute for the Arts (Antwerp University, Belgium) where he leads the Culture Commons Quest Office (CCQO). Gielen is editor of the international book series Antennae–Arts in Society (Valiz). In 2016 he became laureate of the Odysseus grant for excellent international scientific research of the Fund for Scientific Research Flanders in Belgium. In 2022 he was appointed by the Flemish Government as curator of the Culture Talks conference. Gielen has published

many books which have been translated in Chinese, English, Polish, Portuguese, Russian, Spanish, Turkish and Ukrainian. His research focuses on creative labour, the common, urban and cultural politics. Gielen works and lives in Antwerp, Belgium.
www.ccqo.eu
www.uantwerpen.be/en/research-groups/aria/

Mohamed Hijji was a prominent Egyptian designer, artist and illustrator. He collaborated with many publishers in different parts of the Arab world. His book *Shimal, Yemin* is banned, but he made it freely available to the public during the 2011 Egyptian uprising on his social media page after changing its name to *al-'ar* (Shame).

Erwin Jans (1963) studied Germanic Languages and Literatures (Dutch, English, German) and Drama & Theatre at the University of Leuven (Belgium). He worked as a dramaturg at several important theatres in Belgium and the Netherlands. He is currently working at Toneelhuis in Antwerpen. He has been teaching on theatre and drama at several universities and theatre schools in Flanders. He worked with directors such as Ivo van Hove, Wim Vandekeybus, Franz Marijnen and especially Guy Cassiers. He writes extensively on literature, theatre and culture. He is editor in chief of the Flemish literary magazine DW B. He published *Interculturele intoxicaties: Over kunst, cultuur en verschil* (*Intercultural Intoxications: On Art, Culture and Diversity*) (2006). He was co-editor of an anthology of Flemish postwar poetry *Hotel New Flandres* (2008). Together with the philosopher Eric Clemens he wrote an essay on democracy that was also translated in French (2010). He published an anthology of the dramatic work of the Flemish playwright and director Tone Brulin (2017).

Mazen Kerbaj is a Lebanese comics author, visual artist, and musician born in Beirut in 1975. He also works on selective illustration and design projects and has taught at the American University of Beirut. Kerbaj is the author of fifteen books translated into more than ten languages and his work has been shown in

[redacted]

galleries, museums and art fairs around the world. Mazen Kerbaj is widely considered as one of the initiators and key players of the Lebanese free improvisation and experimental music scene. As a trumpet player, he pushes the boundaries of the instrument beyond recognition.

Lara Khaldi is a cultural worker based between Occupied Jerusalem, Palestine and Amsterdam, Netherlands. She was a member of the curatorial team of documenta fifteen/Lumbung (2019–2022) and has been working as artistic director of de Appel, Amsterdam since January 2023. She has co-curated various exhibitions over the years some of which are the Jerusalem show 5 & 6 and Sharjah Biennial 13. She taught at and was the head of the Media Studies Program at Bard Al Quds, Jerusalem 2017–2020. She has also taught at the International Academy of Art, Ramallah, Birzeit University, Palestine and Sandberg Institute, Amsterdam. She is a co-founding member of School of Intrusions and Question of Funding collectives.

Maha Maamoun is an artist, curator and publisher living and working in Cairo. Her work examines the form, function and currency of popular visual and literary images as an entry point to investigating the cultural fabric that we weave and are woven into. She is a co-founder of the Contemporary Image Collective (CIC)—an independent non-profit space for art and culture founded in Cairo in 2004, and co-founder of Kayfa ta, a publishing and curatorial initiative founded in 2012.

Médecins Sans Frontières (MSF) translates to 'doctors without borders'. The organization provides medical assistance to people affected by conflict, epidemics, disasters, or exclusion from healthcare. The teams are made up of tens of thousands of professionals working in health and medical care, logistics, administration, communications, skilled trades—all bound together by our charter and serving people in need. Their actions are guided by medical ethics and the principles of impartiality, independence, and neutrality. They are a non-profit, self-governed, member-based organisation.

Sohail Salem (1974, Gaza) is a visual artist based in Gaza. He earned his Bachelor of Arts in Fine Arts from Al-Aqsa University in 1999, where he later taught art for a year. He is a co-founder of the Eltiqa' Group for Contemporary Arts. Sohail has participated in various residency programs, including the Summer Art Academy at Darat Al Funun, Khalid Shoman Foundation in Amman, under the supervision of the late artist Marwan Qassab Bachi in 2001 and 2003. He also completed residencies at Arts Place de l'Ile in Geneva, Switzerland, in 2005, and at the Cité Internationale des Arts in Paris, France, in 2010. Suhail's artistic practice encompasses design, installation art, sculpture, photography, and graphic design, with a focus on capturing nature and human activities.

Roschanack Shaery-Yazdi received her PhD in Middle Eastern Studies at the University of Chicago and is an associate professor at the University of Antwerp. She fled Iran in 1986 amid the Iran-Iraq war to Germany and sought refuge in the very country that enriched itself by supplying Iraq with bombs. Due to her life between these contrasting worlds, she has become interested in questions of intersectionality and structural inequality. Her teaching, writing, and private life have centred on contemplations and practices aimed at healing the wounds that white supremacist structures and their entitled attitudes in daily interactions have inflicted on her ancestors and on communities across the Middle East. Others may refer to these healing activities as decolonization, unlearning, disobedience, and resistance.

Bahia Shehab is a multidisciplinary artist, designer, political activist and historian whose work focuses on the interaction and intersection of modern identity and ancient cultural heritage. Her imaginative combination of calligraphy and Islamic art history produced cutting edge, beautiful, impactful street art during the Arab Spring and continues to inform her work as an educator and designer.

Having always been concerned with identity and preserving cultural heritage, she investigates art history to reinterpret contemporary Arab politics, feminist discourse and social

[redacted]

issues. Her culturally oriented work enables her to use history as a means to better understand the present and find solutions for the future.
www.bahiashehab.com

Theatre collective *STAN*, an acronym for Stop Thinking About Names, was founded in 1989 by Jolente De Keersmaeker, Damiaan De Schrijver, Waas Gramser, and Frank Vercruyssen, who met at the Antwerp Conservatory.

STAN operates on the belief that theatre is not an elitist art form but rather a critical reflection on how we live, our convictions, concerns, and indignation. Each member of STAN is part of the collective while also pursuing their own artistic path. The search for shared affinities goes hand in hand with the necessity to collaborate and interact with guest performers and other companies.
www.stan.be

Walid Taher (1969) is an Egyptian author, designer of children's books, plastic artist and journalist painter. He has published more than forty children's books, including *The Black Spot*, *Seven Souls* and *The Island of Sailor Barakat*.

Jana Traboulsi is an artist, designer, and academic. She serves as Assistant Professor of Graphic Design at the American University of Beirut. She co-founded and is Creative Director of the pan-Arab quarterly *Bidayat* and is the Artistic Director of Snoubar Bayrout Publishing House. Jana is also the co-founder of *Sigil*, an art collective in Beirut and New York, and *The Laab*, a critical and creative unit exploring the intersection of art and politics. Her recent exhibitions include her participation in *and from my heart I blow kisses to the sea and houses* at the 24th Triennale Milano (2025, Award for Best International Pavilion). She co-edited *A Collapsing Lexicon* (2023).

Emily Van Driessen (1995) is an independent writer, curator, and art mediator. She studied Translation and Cultural Studies. Her practice focuses on writing and curating (audio)visual arts in experimental contexts beyond the traditional gallery space. Recent publications include: 'Painting Through Violence: A Conversation with Diana Al-Halabi', *Art Rotterdam* (2025, ongoing collaboration); 'Welt am Draht: A Tapestry of Meanings', *GalleryViewer Magazine* (2025, ongoing collaboration); 'Dating an Art Fair' and 'Meditating with Mark Rothko', *How to Art* (2025, ongoing). Recent projects include: upcoming exhibition with Willem de Haan, Havenhuis Port of Antwerp-Bruges, Antwerp, 2026; co-curated exhibition and performance on a lake, MEERMEER, Bruges, 2024. Van Driessen lives and works in Antwerp.

Frank Vercruyssen (1965) is a founding member of Belgian theatre company TG STAN, working within this company since 1989, performing in Dutch, French and English. These past years he co-created and appeared in, among others, *Nora*, *The Cherry Orchard*, *The Monkey Trial*, *Infidèles*, *Poquelin II* and *Mitya*.

He created several performances with young Belgian and foreign actors and dancers, such as *The Tangible*, *Mademoiselle Else* and *Scènes de la vie conjugale*, appeared in a number of movies and television series and regularly teaches in theatre and dance schools in Belgium and abroad.

Annelys de Vet (1974) is a Belgium-based designer, researcher, and educator. She completed her PhD at Sint Lucas Antwerp/ARIA (2024) with the dissertation *Disarming Design: Politics of Participatory Practices*, and currently teaches in the MA Context: Socio-Political program at Sint Lucas School of Arts, Antwerp. From 2020 to 2022, she led the temporary master's Disarming Design at the Sandberg Instituut, Amsterdam. Her practice focuses on participatory design in socio-political contexts, conflict, and resilience. She is the founder of the publishing platform Subjective Editions and co-founder of the design label Disarming Design from Palestine. De Vet lives and works near Brussels.

Saadi Youssef (1934–2021) was an Iraqi author, poet, journalist, publisher, and political activist. He published thirty volumes of poetry in addition to seven books of prose.

Gamlet Zinkivskyi (1986) is an artist, known for his street art works and illustrations, and also works in the field of painting, graphics, art books, and photography. He studied at the Kharkiv Art School and the Kharkiv Academy of Design and Arts, at the Faculty of Monumental Painting. He was expelled from the academy in 2009 for academic arrears in physical education and psychology. In 2013, together with Zhanna Kadyrova and Mykola Rydny, he represented Ukraine at the 53rd Venice Biennale. Nowadays he lives and works in Kharkiv.

Design and Publishing

Metahaven (book design). The work of Metahaven encompasses design, filmmaking, and writing.
www.instagram.com/metahaven

Valiz is an independent international publisher on contemporary art, theory, critique, design and urban affairs. Our books offer critical reflection and interdisciplinary inspiration and often establish a connection between cultural disciplines and socio-political questions. We publish these books out of our commitment to their content, to artistic and social issues and to the artists, designers and authors. Apart from publishing, Valiz organizes lectures, debates and other cultural projects in which certain topics in contemporary art are explored.
www.valiz.nl

Arts in *Society*

Antennae-Arts *in* Society is a peer-reviewed book series that validates artistic, critical, speculative and essayistic writing as a full academic publishing method. Contributions to the series look upon the arts as 'antennae', feelers for the cultural interpretation and articulation of topical political, economic, social, technological or environmental issues.

The books in this series bring together audiences of diverse backgrounds: artists and other creative makers, academics and researchers from various disciplines, critics, writers, journalists, politicians, curators, and institutional parties, who wish to broaden their view in different political, social and other contexts.

Proposals for book concepts in all artistic and scientific disciplines that take culture as the base of interpretation for the social fabric of our contemporary lives are welcomed and will be considered for publication by the academic board.

Editorial board Valiz-Arts in *Society book series*

Indices

Index of Names

Aboriginal Tent Embassy, Canberra AU 138
Ábrego García, Kilmar 287
Abu Elouf, Samar 77
Abu Jihad (Khalil al-Wazir) 30, 213–214, 218
Abusal, Mohamed 178
Adorno, Theodor 209
Agamben, Giorgio 212, 287
Ajjour, Mahmoud 77
Al-Assad, Bashar 60
Al-Bayati, Abdul Wahhab 161–162
Al-Fasa'il, publication, Cairo EG 273
Al-Halabi, Diana 27–28, 135–145
Al-Kitaba al-'Ukhra, Cairo EG 273–274
Al-Malaika, Nazik 296–297
Al-Nawwab, Muzaffar 169–170
Al-Qasim, Samih 173–175
Al-Sabbagh, Mohamed 273
Al-Sayyab, Badr Shakir 157–158, 296
Al-Tatawur, Cairo EG 273–274, 281
Amnesty International 286
Arafat, Yasser 213
Arendt, Hannah 44–45, 53, 78
Art and Liberty Group, EG 273
Art Rotterdam, NL 138–139
Ashkar, Amir 28, 31, 192–197
Asociación para la Recuperación de la Memoria Histórica (Association for the Recovery of Historical Memory, ARMH), ES 248–250
Azabal, Lubna 110
Azzam, Tammam 25, 29, 58–65

Bancroft Library, University of California, Berkeley US 277
Barthes, Roland 246, 255–256
Basset, Bob (Serhii Petrov) 29, 204, 208–209
Beddegenoodts, Jan 27, 29, 52–54
Beirut Art Center (BAC), LB 275–279
Ben Chikha, Chokri 52
Benfquih, Yousra 24–25
Ben Gurion Airport, Lod/Tel Aviv IL 141
Benjamin, Walter 82–83, 248, 257
Berliner Ensemble, DE 108
Bernhard, Thomas 107, 111–113
Binoche, Juliette 89
Boss, Pauline 247
Bourdieu, Pierre 124
Brecht, Bertolt 104–111, 124, 138
Bredekamp, Horst 256
Brueghel, Pieter 110
Bubu (parakeet) 134
Butler, Judith 26, 84–85, 251, 253, 289

Calvet Martínez, Elisenda 247
Cella, Bernhard 275–277
Centro Internacional de Memoria y Derechos Humanos (CIEMEDH), ES 259
Chaplin, Charlie 113
Chomsky, Noam 126, 286
Choukri, Mohamed 273
Cools, Guy 289
Cultural Development Fund, EG 274

Damascus University, SY 60, 297
Darwish, Mahmoud 165–167, 211, 221
David de Lossy, Julie 26, 94–99
De Cock, Bruno 26, 94–100
De Geest, Laura 111
De Keersmaeker, Jolente 120, 122, 124, 126
De Munck, Marlies 26, 28, 31
Derrida, Jacques 87, 256
De Schrijver, Damiaan 120–126
Dessau, Paul 111
De Sutter, Koen 110
De Wever, Bart 89
Dewinter, Filip 42
Dewispelaere, Tom 111
Documenta, Kassel DE 178
Dosch, Laetitia 110
Dulle Griet 110

Egge, Mr. 104–105
Eichmann, Adolf 44, 78
Eilif 110–111
Eltiqa Gallery, Gaza City PS 178–179
El-Wardany, Haytham 274
El Zein Khoury, Joumana 77
Espinosa Maestre, Francisco 247
Esslin, Martin 109
Estaras, Lisi 110
European Parliament 29, 204
Ezzat, Amr 279

Fanon, Frantz 144
Fatah, PS 213
Fattal, Simone 277
FC Bergman, BE 113-114
Fogiel Lewin, Naama Shoshana 30
Franco, Alain 111
Franco, Francisco 31, 246, 248, 254-255
Fraser, Nancy 46, 48
Freud, Sigmund 124
Frontex 286-287

Gallery 68, Cairo EG 272, 274
García Diaz, Lara 31
Gaza Soup Kitchen, PS 85-87
Geoactivismo.org 249
Gharib, Samir 274
Gibran, Gibran Khalil 185
Goya, Francisco de 61
Grimonprez, Johan 51, 53
Grossman, David 78-79
Groys, Boris 215, 218

Habibi, Emile 216
Hamas, PS 42, 78-80, 113
Hamoudi 86
Han, Byung-Chul 288
Happel, Joeri 110
Harney, Stefano 215
Hassouna, Fatima 88-89
Henein, George 273
Hertmans, Stefan 47
Herzog, Yitzhak 14
Hijji, Mohamed 28-29, 148, 150, 154, 158, 162, 166, 170, 174
Himmler, Heinrich 112
Hitler, Adolf 108, 120
Höller, Clara 112
Höller, Rudolf 112
Höller, Vera 112
Honigmann, Heddy 53
Houbrechts, Lisaboa 107, 109-111
Horizon Europe 44
Human Rights League 286
Hussein al-Adawy, Ali 281

IDF (Israel Defence Forces) 178, 218, 229
Ibsen, Henrik 120
Isleyen, Aydin 110-111

Jans, Erwin 26-27
Jesus Christ 10
Kamel, Anwar 273-274, 281
Kattrin 110
Kayfa ta 270-271, 275-281
Kazerne Dossin, Mechelen BE 76
Kerbaj, Mazen 26, 29, 68-72
Keshta, Hisham 273-274
Keuner, Mr. 104-106
Khaldi, Lara 29-30
Klimt, Gustav 62
Kubrick, Stanley 76

Louvre, Musée du 213, 215

Magnum Photos 46
Mansour, Ibrahim 272
Mapas de Memoria (Memory Maps), ES 254, 259
Marx, Karl 108, 124
Massad, Joseph 221
Mayenburg, Marius von 120
Medea 110
Médecins Sans Frontières (MSF) (Doctors Without Borders) 94-98, 298
Metallica 29, 209
Mielants, Tim 76
Milgram, Stanley 78
Mitchell, Timothy 217
MMAG foundation, Amman JO 275
Mondriaan Fund 134
Moreno Andrés, Jorge 248, 255-256
Mossad, Tel Aviv IL 214
Moten, Fred 215
Mother Courage (Anna Fierling) 107-110
Mouffe, Chantal 115
Muftaqir, Mustafa 153-154

Nashif, Esmail 219
Netanyahu, Benjamin 24, 45
NY Art Book Fair, US 275

Odysseus 105
Olyslaegers, Jeroen 47

Palacios González, Daniel 250-251, 253
Palestine Liberation Organization, PS 213
Panizo, Laura Marina 252-253
Pinochet, Augusto 253

Post-Apollo Press, Sausalito US 277, 279
Pottier, Yvette 111
Proust, Marcel 255
Putin, Vladimir 24

Quadrino, Pietro 110

Rancière, Jacques 98
Registro Nacional de Personas Desaparecidas y No Localizadas (National Register of Disappeared and Missing Persons), MX 249

Saeed 216
Said, Edward 14
Salazar, Andrade 254
Salem, Sohail 28, 176, 178–189
Samuel, Julia 289
Schweizerkas 110
Shaery-Yazdi, Roschanack 31, 242
Shawri, Mawda 32, 286–289
Shostakovich, Dmitri Dmitriyevich 120
Slipknot, US 29, 209
Sontag, Susan 26, 41, 43, 52–53, 80–85, 87, 89, 95, 122
Stalin, Joseph 120
STAN (Stop Thinking About Names), BE 27, 120–127
Steyerl, Hito 212
Stieglitz, Alfred 88
Strand, Paul 88
Swedish Army Museum, Stockholm SE 200

Taher, Walid 20–21, 34–35, 128–129, 222–223, 292
Taqa, Shadhil 296
The Question of Funding 179, 302
Toneelhuis, Antwerp BE 27, 107, 115, 301
Traboulsi, Jana 31, 262–266, 292
Trump, Donald 24, 106, 114, 200, 287
Tzuc, Efraín 249

United Nations 249
Universidad Nacional de Educación a Distancia (UNED), Madrid ES 259
University of Antwerp, BE 42, 299, 300, 303

Vanbesien, Robin 32, 288–289
Vance, J.D. 209
Van Driessen, Emily 27
Vercruyssen, Frank 120, 122–123, 125–126, 304
Vet, Annelys de 28
Violence (character) 104–105
Vishmidt, Marina 217

Warehouse421, Abu Dhabi AE 275–276
Weber, Max 43
Weigel, Helene 108
Wekker, Gloria 145
Wils, Emmy 120
Woolf, Virginia 81
World Press Photo 77

Yasser Arafat Museum, Ramallah PS 213–215
Yerma 110
Younis, Ala 270

Youssef, Saadi 149–151

Zelensky, Volodymyr 209
Zinkivskyi, Gamlet 28, 200–208
Zinn, Howard 126

Index of Places

Abu Dhabi AE 275
Afghanistan 84
Aleppo SY 61
Al-Rimal, Gaza City PS 185
Al Zawaydah PS 86
Amman JO 270, 275, 303
Antwerp BE 27, 32, 76, 107, 120, 301
Argentina 139
Austria 112

Beirut LB 142, 277, 296, 301
Belgium 47, 286, 298, 299, 300, 301, 305
Berlin DE 25, 60, 297
Brussels BE 29, 204, 298, 300, 305
Bucha UA 114

Cairo EG 32, 135, 270, 273, 302
Calais FR 96, 98

California US 277
Capitol Hill, Washington D.C. US 9
Castile-La Mancha ES 248
Catalonia ES-CT 252
Chile 252
Colombia 250
Congo 123, 125

Damascus SY 60, 296, 297
Deir al-Balah PS 185, 187–188
Denmark 108
Dubai AE 61, 297

East Berlin DDR 108
Egypt 281
Erez IL 214
Europe 10, 40, 45, 65, 107–108, 125, 141, 200–201, 204, 235–236, 238–240, 286–287, 289, 297

France 231, 303

Gaza City PS 178, 185, 186
Gaza PS 14, 25, 31, 40, 42, 68, 76–77, 79, 84–85, 88–89, 97, 106–107, 113–114, 121, 123, 140–142, 178, 185–186, 214, 219–220, 234, 236, 264, 266, 279, 303
Germany 45, 104, 112–114, 125, 179, 234, 303
Guernica ES-PV 113, 115

Hungary 125

Iran 234–235, 303
Iraq 140, 303
Israel 31, 40, 45, 52, 79, 84, 89, 106, 113–114, 135, 236–238, 266

Jordan 65

Kassel DE 178
Kharkiv UA 28, 200–202, 205–206, 306

Latin America 249
Lebanon 25, 98, 134, 141
León SP 248
Libya 287

Mechelen BE 76, 300
Mexico 249
Middle East 10
Mons/Bergen BE 286

Netherlands, the 27, 134, 137, 139, 142, 144, 301, 302

Palestine 25, 42, 44–45, 47–50, 137–139, 141, 179, 213, 218, 221, 230, 237, 302
Paris FR 274, 303
Priaranza del Bierzo ES 248
Ramallah PS 213–214, 302
Rotterdam NL 134, 138, 143, 296
Russia 40, 200

Sausalito US 277
Scandinavia 108
Schuman Square, Brussels BE 9
Sheikh Jarrah, Jerusalem PS 137
South Africa 106
Spain 31, 246, 248
Srebrenica BA 53
Stockholm SE 200
Sudan 97
Sweden 108
Syria 61

Tangiers MA 273
Tantoura PS 216
Tehran IR 235
Tunisia 148
Tunis TN 214
Turkey 125, 287
Troy, Ancient Greece 120

Ukraine 24–25, 40, 42, 48–50, 107, 113, 123, 200–205, 212, 306
United Kingdom 286
United States 40, 108, 125, 238, 277, 287

Vietnam 84, 140

Weimar Republic 104
West Bank PS 76

Yugoslavia 84

Colophon

Colophon

In the Absence of Bombs
Art, War, and Silence

Editors
Pascal Gielen, Bahia Shehab

Authors
Amir Ashkar, Jan Beddegenoodts, Yousra Benfquih, Marlies De Munck, Naama Shoshana Fogiel Lewin, Lara García Diaz, Pascal Gielen, Mohamed Hijji, Erwin Jans, Mazen Kerbaj, Lara Khaldi, Maha Maamoun, Sohail Salem, Roschanack Shaery-Yazdi, Bahia Shehab, Walid Taher, Jana Traboulsi, Emily Van Driessen, Annelys de Vet

Antennae-Arts *in* Society Series n° 32 by Valiz, Amsterdam

Copy editing
Dutton Hauhart

Translations
Poems in the works of Mohamed Hijji – Bahia Shehab

Proofreading and indices
Jacinta van de Ven

Design
Metahaven

Paper interior
Munken Print 100 gr 1.5

Paper cover
Munken Pure 240 gr

Lithography
Wilco Art Books, Amersfoort

Printing and binding
Wilco Art Books, Amersfoort

Project editor Valiz
Eli Witteman

Publisher
Valiz, Amsterdam, 2025
Astrid Vorstermans
www.valiz.nl

This publication was made possible through the generous support of

Vfonds, Utrecht

Mondriaan Fund, Amsterdam

ISBN 978-94-93246-59-1

Distribution

BE: EPO, *www.epo.be*
USA/Canada/Latin America: D.A.P., *www.artbook.com*
GB/IE: Central Books, *www.centralbooks.com*
BE/NL/LU: Centraal Boekhuis, *www.cb.nl*
Europe/Asia: Idea Books, *www.ideabooks.nl*
Australia: Perimeter Books, *www.perimeterdistribution.com*

ISBN 978-94-93246-59-1

Printed and bound in the Netherlands

[redacted]

Antennae Series

Antennae N° 1
The Fall of the Studio
Artists at Work
edited by Wouter Davidts & Kim Paice
Amsterdam: Valiz, 2009
(2nd ed.: 2010),
ISBN 978-90-78088-29-5

Antennae N° 2
Take Place
Photography and Place
from Multiple Perspectives
edited by Helen Westgeest
Amsterdam: Valiz, 2009,
ISBN 978-90-78088-35-6

Antennae N° 3
The Murmuring of the
Artistic Multitude
Global Art, Memory and Post-Fordism
Pascal Gielen (author)
Arts *in* Society
Amsterdam: Valiz, 2009
(2nd ed.: 2011),
ISBN 978-90-78088-34-9

Antennae N° 4
Locating the Producers
Durational Approaches to Public Art
edited by Paul O'Neill
& Claire Doherty
Amsterdam: Valiz, 2011,
ISBN 978-90-78088-51-6

Antennae N° 5
Community Art
The Politics of Trespassing
edited by Paul De Bruyne &
Pascal Gielen
Arts *in* Society
Amsterdam: Valiz, 2011
(2nd ed.: 2013),
ISBN 978-90-78088-50-9

Antennae N° 6
See it Again, Say it Again
The Artist as Researcher
edited by Janneke Wesseling
Amsterdam: Valiz, 2011,
ISBN 978-90-78088-53-0

Antennae N° 7
Teaching Art in the
Neoliberal Realm
Realism versus Cynicism
edited by Pascal Gielen &
Paul De Bruyne
Arts *in* Society
Amsterdam: Valiz, 2012
(2nd ed.: 2013),
ISBN 978-90-78088-57-8

Antennae N° 8
Institutional Attitudes
Instituting Art in a Flat World
edited by Pascal Gielen
Arts *in* Society
Amsterdam: Valiz, 2013,
ISBN 978-90-78088-68-4

Antennae N° 9
Dread
The Dizziness of Freedom
edited by Juha van 't Zelfde
Amsterdam: Valiz, 2013,
ISBN 978-90-78088-81-3

Antennae N° 10
Participation Is Risky
Approaches to Joint Creative Processes
edited by Liesbeth Huybrechts
Amsterdam: Valiz, 2014,
ISBN 978-90-78088-77-6

Antennae N° 11
The Ethics of Art
Ecological Turns in the Performing Arts
edited by Guy Cools & Pascal Gielen
Arts *in* Society
Amsterdam: Valiz, 2014,
ISBN 978-90-78088-87-5

Antennae N° 12
Alternative Mainstream
Making Choices in Pop Music
Gert Keunen (author)
Arts *in* Society
Amsterdam: Valiz, 2014,
ISBN 978-90-78088-95-0

Antennae N° 13
The Murmuring of the Artistic Multitude
Global Art, Politics and Post-Fordism
Pascal Gielen (author)
Completely revised and enlarged edition of Antennae N° 3
Arts *in* Society
Amsterdam: Valiz, 2015,
ISBN 978-94-92095-04-6

Antennae N° 14
Aesthetic Justice
Intersecting Artistic and Moral Perspectives
edited by Pascal Gielen & Niels Van Tomme
Arts *in* Society
Amsterdam: Valiz, 2015,
ISBN 978-90-78088-86-8

Antennae N° 15
No Culture, No Europe
On the Foundation of Politics
edited by Pascal Gielen
Arts *in* Society
Amsterdam: Valiz, 2015,
ISBN 978-94-92095-03-9

Antennae N° 16
Arts Education Beyond Art
Teaching Art in Times of Change
edited by Barend van Heusden & Pascal Gielen
Arts *in* Society
Amsterdam: Valiz, 2015,
ISBN 978-90-78088-85-1

Antennae N° 17
Mobile Autonomy
Exercises in Artists' Self-Organization
edited by Nico Dockx & Pascal Gielen
Arts *in* Society
Amsterdam: Valiz, 2015,
ISBN 978-94-92095-10-7

Antennae N° 18
Moving Together
Theorizing and Making Contemporary Dance
Rudi Laermans (author)
Arts *in* Society
Amsterdam: Valiz, 2015,
ISBN 978-90-78088-52-3

Antennae N° 19
Spaces for Criticism
Shifts in Contemporary Art Discourses
edited by Thijs Lijster, Suzana Milevska, Pascal Gielen, Ruth Sonderegger
Arts *in* Society
Amsterdam: Valiz, 2015,
ISBN 978-90-78088-75-2

Antennae N° 20
Interrupting the City
Artistic Constitutions of the Public Sphere
edited by Sander Bax, Pascal Gielen & Bram Ieven
Arts *in* Society
Amsterdam: Valiz, 2015,
ISBN 978-94-92095-02-2

Antennae N° 21
In-between Dance Cultures
On the Migratory Artistic Identity of Sidi Larbi Cherkaoui and Akram Khan
Guy Cools (author)
Arts *in* Society
Amsterdam: Valiz, 2015,
ISBN 978-94-92095-11-4

Antennae N° 22
Imaginative Bodies
Dialogues in Performance Practices
Guy Cools (author)
Arts *in* Society
Amsterdam: Valiz, 2016,
ISBN 978-94-92095-20-6

Antennae N° 23
The Practice of Dramaturgy
Working on Actions in Performance
edited by Konstantina Georgelou, Efrosini Protopapa, Danae Theodoridou
Arts *in* Society
Amsterdam: Valiz, 2017,
ISBN: 978-94-92095-18-3

Antennae N° 24
The Art of Civil Action
Political Space and Cultural Dissent
edited by Philipp Dietachmair, Pascal Gielen
Arts *in* Society
Amsterdam: Valiz, 2017,
ISBN: 978-94-92095-39-8

Antennae N° 25
Commonism
A New Aesthetics of the Real
Nico Dockx & Pascal Gielen (authors)
Arts *in* Society
Amsterdam: Valiz, 2018,
ISBN 978-94-92095-47-3

Antennae N° 26
The Future of the New
Artistic Innovation in Times of Social Acceleration
edited by Thijs Lijster
Arts *in* Society
Amsterdam: Valiz, 2018,
ISBN 978-94-92095-58-9

Antennae N° 27
Contemporary Artist Residencies
Reclaiming Time and Space
edited by Taru Elfving, Pascal Gielen, Irmeli Kokko
Arts *in* Society
Amsterdam: Valiz, 2019,
ISBN 978-94-92095-46-6

Antennae N° 28
When Fact Is Fiction
Documentary Art in the Post-Truth Era
edited by Nele Wynants
Arts *in* Society
Amsterdam: Valiz, 2020,
ISBN 978-94-92095-71-8

Antennae N° 29
The Aesthetics of Ambiguity
Understanding and Addressing Monoculture
edited by Pascal Gielen & Nav Haq
Arts *in* Society
Amsterdam: Valiz, 2020,
ISBN 978-94-92095-76-3

Antennae N° 30
Performing Mourning
Laments in Contemporary Art
Guy Cools (author)
Arts *in* Society
Amsterdam: Valiz, 2021,
ISBN 978-94-92095-98-5

Antennae N° 31
Sensing Earth
Cultural Quests Across a Heated Globe
edited by Philipp Dietachmair, Pascal Gielen, Georgia Nicolau
Arts in Society
Amsterdam: Valiz, 2023,
ISBN 978-94-93246-24-9